CW00866483

The Strangers Among Us

Tales from a Global Migrant Worker Movement

Edited by

Joseph B. Atkins

A LabourStart Book

Copyright © 2016 *LabourStart*

David Bacon chapter, copyright reserved for David Bacon.

All rights reserved.

ISBN: 1523355603
ISBN-13: 978-1523355600

Cover photo courtesy of Silvia Giagnoni.

DEDICATION

The Strangers Among Us: Tales from a Global Migrant Labor Movement is dedicated to my late mother, Maria Stoller Atkins (1921-2014). She was an immigrant herself, a German native (once imprisoned by the Gestapo) who followed her G.I. husband, my father, to America after World War II. She had been a stenographer in Germany, and she worked as a seamstress in the U.S. South much of my childhood. She struggled through hard work, homesickness, and, early on, anti-German bias to make a home for her family. She taught me about philosophy, classical music, the evil of prejudice, and the world beyond my immediate horizons in the very insulated South.

Joseph B. Atkins

CONTENTS

ACKNOWLEDGMENTS

This book was years in the making, and many people have helped tremendously along the way. Of course, my wife, Suzanne Centenio Atkins, deserves much credit for keeping the faith throughout and helping me with computer and other issues that came up. We traveled together to such far-flung locales as Singapore, Taipei, Hong Kong, Beijing, and Buenos Aires, where I was able to do key research and reporting for this book. Any list of others who helped make *The Strangers Among Us* a reality is bound to be incomplete, but here are some of those I want to be sure to acknowledge:

Publisher and writer Eric Lee and *LabourStart*, Daniel Blackburn, Bill Chandler, Nancy Yan Xu, and all the writers who contributed words, ideas, and photographs to The Strangers Among Us, Bob Guccione Jr., Eric Stark, Wieslaw Oleksy, Pavol Mudry, Brian Finnegan, and the University of Mississippi and Meek School of Journalism and New Media.

Contributors to *The Strangers Among Us: Tales from a Global Migrant Worker Movement*

Bill Chandler is executive director of the internationally recognized Mississippi Immigrants Rights Alliance and a veteran labor activist who worked with Cesar Chavez and the United Farm Workers on the frontlines in the 1960s. He was a key organizer in the 1966 farm workers strike in Texas' Rio Grande Valley and subsequent consumer boycott across Texas and the South. Chandler was named a Purpose Prize Fellow in 2009.

Joseph B. Atkins, a veteran journalist, labor writer, and professor of journalism at the University of Mississippi. He is the author of *Covering for the Bosses: Labor and the Southern Press* (University Press of Mississippi, 2008) and the novel *Casey's Last Chance* (Sartoris Literary Group, 2015), and editor/contributing writer of *The Mission: Journalism, Ethics and the World* (Iowa State University Press, 2002).

David Bacon is an award-winning documentary photographer and writer as well as veteran labor organizer and immigrant rights activist. He is the author of *Illegal People* (Beacon Press, 2008), and his latest book is *The Right to Stay Home* (Beacon Press, 2013), which discusses alternatives to forced migration and the criminalization of migrants. His articles have appeared in the *Los Angeles Times, Nation* and other publications.

Silvia Giagnoni, an associate professor in the Department of Communication and Theatre at Auburn University Montgomery, is author of *Fields of Resistance: The Struggle of Florida's Farmworkers for Justice* (Haymarket Books, 2011) and *Oltre la Siepe. Alla Ricerca di Harper Lee* (Trans. *Beyond the Hedge. In Search of Harper Lee*) (Roma: Edizioni dell'Asino, 2013). A native of Italy, Giagnoni is currently finishing her book on new immigrants and immigration in Alabama in the age of HB56 (forthcoming NewSouth Press).

Eric Lee is the founding editor of *LabourStart*, the news and campaigning website of the international trade union movement. He is the author of several books, including *The Labour Movement and the Internet: The New Internationalism* and the forthcoming *Democratic Socialism: The Georgian Experiment*.

Daniel Blackburn is director of the International Centre for Trade Union Rights in London, England, and editor of the organization's flagship journal, *International Union Rights*. An attorney as well as a specialist in international labor law, Blackburn has lectured around the world on human and worker rights.

Angie Hsu is a local activist in south Tel Aviv, Israel, the city area most densely populated by migrant workers and asylum seekers/refugees. After working with Migrants' Rights Network as a graduate student at the London School of Economics, Hsu joined the staff at Kav LaOved - Worker's Hotline, the most recognized organization promoting and protecting the labor rights of all workers in Israel, including those of Palestinians, migrant workers and asylum seekers/refugees.

Sindhu Menon is a labor journalist who has written for *Labour File* in New Delhi, India, *Equal Times, International Union Rights*, and other publications.

Nancy Yan Xu is an award-winning journalist born in China and living in Los Angeles. She is chief editor/general manager of the U.S. edition of *Global Times*, one of China's top daily newspapers, in both English and Chinese languages. She is also co-author of *Boundary Stones of China* (Hong Kong China News Publication, 2008) and *Eve to Civil Society* (Hong Kong China News Publication, 2007).

Takehiko Kambayashi is an author and veteran journalist who serves as Tokyo, Japan, correspondent for the German Press Agency (DPA). He has written for the *Christian Science Monitor, Washington Times*, and *The Diplomat*. Among his wide range of blue-collar jobs before his journalism career was service as waiter to Japan's prime minister and Imperial Family.

Bill Chandler, executive director of the Mississippi Immigrants Rights Alliance in Jackson, Mississippi, USA. *Photo credit: Joseph B. Atkins.*

FOREWORD

By

Bill Chandler

Executive Director, Mississippi Immigrants Rights Alliance

Butterflies and swallows and flamingos have forever spread their wings to flee the cold, the way whales swim in search of other seas and salmon and trout seek out their rivers. Year after year, they all travel thousands of miles on the open roads of air and water.

The roads of human flight, however, are not free.

In immense caravans they march, fugitives fleeing their unbearable lives.

They travel from south to north and from rising sun to setting sun.

Their place in the world has been stolen. They have been stripped of their work and their land. Many flee wars, but many more ruinous wages and exhausted plots of land.

These pilgrims, shipwrecked by globalization, wander about, unearthing roads, seeking homes, knocking on doors that swing open when money calls but otherwise slam shut in their faces. Some manage to sneak in. Others arrive as corpses that the sea delivers to the forbidden shore, or as nameless bodies buried in the world they hoped to reach.

– Eduardo Galeano, in Voices of Time, A Life in Stories

     Out of Africa our ancestors came some 100,000 years ago following coast lines and water ways for tens of thousands of years.   Crossing no borders these migrants sought safety, sustenance, and survival.

Settling in new environments over tens of thousands of years, they established communities and belief systems to explain their environments.   Changing climates, over-population, soil depletion, lack of water and food, violence and wars pushed them onward into lands we now call Europe, Asia, and Australia, into the Pacific and the American hemisphere. Cultures developed with their hierarchies, settlements and villages became cities and city states in Africa, Asia, Europe and the Americas often unaware of each other.

Trade developed between the cultures evolving from the earliest exchanges between communities. The power hungry and greedy competed and fought over territory, wealth and resources, empires were built and destroyed.   "Borders" with fences, walls and gates staked out the elite's territory, often without regard to the people who lived on the land.   Europeans used their technology to travel to "discover" other peoples and to enslave them and appropriate their wealth and resources.

New borders were drawn again without regard to the people who lived there.   Beginning with the Americas and into Asia and Africa, the imperialistic Europeans attempted to claim the Earth as their own.   Portugal, Spain, England, the French, the Germans and the Dutch, among others, carved up the world for their own profit.   People of the Global South were forced to do the bidding of the North.

During the last century and before, the Middle East, Africa, and parts of Asia were coveted. Following the "Great War" (World War I), the French and English attempted to colonize those peoples. With the destruction of industrial Europe and Asia, the United States actively entered the fray rationalizing "Manifest Destiny" as its right to control the Western Hemisphere. Puerto Rico, Hawaii, the Philippines, and others were seized.   People throughout the world fought back against the colonizers-- politically and violently--in various and often rival movements.

When the United States seized half of the territory of Mexico, the people living there became victims of the same system of exploitation as the people kidnapped from Africa and forced into labor to build the economies for white European elites who had conquered much of the continent. This history sets the stage for the current system of exploiting workers of color from the South for the benefit of the North that we've experienced during the last century and a half.

Following the U.S. Civil War, newly "freed" Africans were violently pushed back into forced labor on plantations and mines throughout the U.S. South. No longer property, they had no "value" except for the products of their work, which went to the whites. Apartheid was the official policy toward Africans in the United States and was applied to the Mexicans there as well. Terrorism ruled. Some 4,000 lynchings of Africans were documented. A nearly equal number of Mexicans in the United States were murdered during the same period. White workers were taught to disdain their co-workers of color and keep them apart.

Chinese workers were recruited to build the railroads and join the Mexicans in the mines of the West. When their work was done, they were attacked and deported. The Chinese Exclusion Act was signed into law. Mexicans were recruited for the mines, farms and ranches, and periodically rounded up and deported regardless of citizenship. A U.S.-born Mexican union organizer I know, with generations of U.S. citizen ancestors before him, often said, "I didn't cross the border—the border crossed me!"

The poverty of the Global South and the wealth of the Global North have made manipulations of the labors of the poor the gold for the rich. Throughout the world complicated but deadly systems have been created to harness workers into a sophisticated culture of exploitation. This is no accident, it is well planned. In this hemisphere, various "free trade" agreements imposed primarily by the United States have hollowed out the economies of much of Mexico and Central America, forcing desperate workers north from their farms to find work to support their families. In their wake, agribusiness conglomerates have appropriated their land for their own benefit. And well-organized and violently competing drug trade routes grew to nourish the insatiable drug use in the United States.

The campaign over the years to enact "Comprehensive Immigration Reform" in the United States has not produced legislation based on human and labor rights. It has been a thinly veiled effort to further codify immigration laws that were never "broken" and cleverly designed to manipulate the U.S. workforce.

Volumes can be written about how the world elite uses these workers. Often far from their countries of origin and their families, not only are they impoverished but millions are sickened and die from their efforts. Their loved ones may never hear from them. Up from Mexico, Central America, Europe and North Africa, the Middle East, and Asia, the stories that follow tell of the struggles of migrant workers to fight back against the systems that exploit their work and attempt to keep them powerless.

While butterflies, swallows and flamingos flow across borders, and capital flows as equally unimpaired as the butterflies, workers are contained by borders and only released as necessary as guest workers or the undocumented to better exploit and serve the wealthy.

INTRODUCTION

An Under-the-Radar Labor Movement Taking Root in the Global South

By

Joseph B. Atkins

Professor of Journalism, University of Mississippi, USA

BADE CITY, Taiwan – A 35-year-old factory worker, his black jacket and khaki pants frayed from wear, tries to tell the long, complex story of his journey from central Vietnam to this industrial city an hour's drive southwest of Taipei. He speaks softly, hesitantly. Next to him is his translator, Father Peter Nguyen Cuong, 52, a Maryknoll priest who himself escaped Vietnam in a small boat decades ago.

He tells me his name but asks that I do not use it. He fears retribution may come to his wife and three children back in Vietnam. "I came here as a worker in a factory in Taipei, a textile factory. I worked for twenty days and I did not get paid, and I left. I had to borrow money for food." [1]

Thousands of dollars in debt to the brokers and contractors who brought him to Taiwan, he moved in with a cousin and eventually found another job. He worked for 40 days but again received no pay. His broker told him he was in trouble with the police because he left his first job without permission. He was a runaway and he must go in hiding, the broker said.

He's one of more than 33,000 migrant workers in Taiwan who have escaped oppressive work conditions and thus are considered illegal. The issue is so serious in Taiwan that the nation's Council on Labor Affairs has called for a migrant runaway law very similar to the Fugitive Slave Law that existed in the United States prior to the Civil War. Under the law, citizens would get rewards for turning in "runaway" workers.

"I came here legal," the factory worker says he told his broker. "Why do I have to run away from the police?"

The police eventually found him and questioned him. They put him in a detention center and told him he still had to pay off his debt and that he would be deported. The first ray of hope came when someone at the detention center suggested he call the Vietnamese Migrant Workers & Brides Office where Father Cuong is executive director. The VMWBO works with unions and other member organizations of the Migrant Empowerment Network in Taiwan (MENT) in the fight for migrant rights in Taiwan.

Attorneys with the VMWBO decided the worker was a victim of human trafficking and agreed to defend his case in court.

"I just want to stay, to have a job, and have money for my family," the factory worker says. "In Vietnam, I worked all kinds of odd jobs to support my family, but the problem is the money. I came here to earn money."

He shakes my hand with both of his and bows as Father Cuong leads him out of the room.

"This is the selling of people," says the priest when he returns. [2]

The VMWBO is ground zero in the battle for the rights of the estimated 70,000 Vietnamese factory and domestic workers in Taiwan. It also fights for the 100,000 Vietnamese women who came here as brides of Taiwanese men and often ended up as little more than sex slaves. "This is the gospel asking you to do for the least of people. Taiwan has them (the workers) because of the low pay," Father Cuong says. "In our shelter now we have thirty people. Some were physically abused, some raped. The domestic workers are more vulnerable. They are not included in the protections of the state labor law."

And yet migrant workers are often scapegoats for societal ills in Taiwan. "Dirty, dangerous, and difficult, the three D's," he says. "No one wants these kinds of jobs, not the Taiwanese, jobs that damage your health, working with chemicals, helping the elderly in nursing homes 24 hours a day.

"We find hope in our faith, in the goodness of hearts. We are not only fighting against other human beings but as witnesses to ourselves. It is very easy to do evil. It's not only here. It's in

Australia, in Japan. They do the same thing everywhere. Here in Taiwan, with the government, if we push hard enough, they begin to care. They want a good image of themselves."

* * *

On the other side of the globe is another worker whose story differs in details but is strikingly similar at its heart.

Diego Reyes Sr., 45, has been traveling the 1,700-mile trek from San Luis Potosi, Mexico, to central North Carolina for half-dozen years, coming in June and staying through early November to pick vegetables, fruit, and tobacco. He works 50 hours a week at $7.25 an hour, sending much of his earnings to his wife and 10 children back home. He was one of the two million Mexican farmers who lost their livelihood after the North American Free Trade Agreement of 1994 allowed subsidized U.S. corn to be dumped on the Mexican market that at times sold for 30 percent below the cost of production.

Reyes lives with five other Latino workers in a rusted-out trailer off Barbecue Road near Sanford, N.C. "Workers have suffered a lot in the field," he says as fans in his trailer hum noisily against the summer heat. [3] Lack of respect is one of the problems. Veterans like himself work for years and help train younger workers but earn the same as someone who has just arrived. Reyes is here legally as part of the so-called H2A guest worker program, but that offers him little protection from exploitation. He is required to stay with his employer and faces deportation or blacklisting if he complains.

"The H-2 guestworker program is fundamentally flawed," according to *Close to Slavery*, a report issued by the Alabama-based Southern Poverty Law Center, and "can be viewed as a modern-day system of indentured servitude." [4]

For such reasons Reyes joined the Farm Labor Organizing Committee (FLOC), which has waged several successful campaigns in recent years to improve the lot of migrant workers who toil long hours for minimal wages, live in substandard housing, and face daily discrimination. "When the grower sees you are a union member, they respect you more," Reyes says. "They give you breaks – some workers get no breaks during the day. You get better treatment, more respect."

Translating his words is his son, Diego Reyes Jr., 21, a seminarian who works for FLOC. "It's not only Sanford, but everywhere, all this propaganda against immigrants. People feel they're stealing their jobs, that immigrants are bad people, drug mules, and criminals. It dehumanizes people. It's not the stealing of jobs. The people came here because of the policies the U.S. implemented in the world." [5]

* * *

The big story within these and similar stories—told to this author during travels across the U.S. South and Global South over the past several years--is the emerging network of support for workers like the Vietnamese migrant in Taiwan and like Diego Reyes Sr., a network that includes but also reaches beyond traditional labor unionism by incorporating churches, non-governmental organizations, and a wide range of community and social groups. Whether by traditional strike, boycott, corporate campaign, or word of mouth, it takes the fight to a broader public, and, although rarely credited in the mainstream media, it often wins.

The new and rising movement takes its inspiration from historical figures like Mahatma Gandhi, who preached corporate responsibility and the idea that capitalists are "trustees" rather than owners of property, and Martin Luther King Jr., a student of Gandhi who died championing the rights of sanitation workers in Memphis, Tenn.

This movement, whether in the U.S. South or Global South, has no single leader and is far from coordinated and interconnected, and many of its member groups may be completely unaware of the others who are part of it. Yet an awareness of it is growing because they are ultimately fighting for the same cause. It's a new social justice movement that takes up the banner for what Father Nguyen calls "the least of people" – those workers, often migrants, who earn the least, are the least protected, and would seem to be the least likely to form a union. By the same token, they are often the most vilified in the countries where they work and blamed for a host of economic and social ills.

"It is easy politics all over the world – blame the foreigner," says John Gee, former president of the Singapore-based Transient Workers Count Too (TWC2) organization. In wealthy Singapore, an economic powerhouse and neoliberal model to the rest of southeast Asia, "the construction sector would grind to a halt without migrant workers. Likewise, the shipyard sector. Probably cleaning services would be badly hit, too, migrant workers provide a substantial minority of the workforce who drive buses, work in shops and restaurants. One in six households have domestic workers... the lowest paid workers of all. Despite complaints by sectors of the public about the presence of foreign workers, most people know that if they were excluded tomorrow, it would be catastrophic for the national economy." [6]

Yet thousands of citizens critical of immigration protested in authoritarian, protest-rare Singapore in early 2013 after a published report indicated government support for a projected 30 percent growth in the country's population by 2030 with migrants constituting half that growth.

Mariane Carnate, 30, a native of The Philippines who has worked as a domestic worker in Hong Kong since 2005, says migrant workers only want to be treated fairly. She works 10 to 12 hours a day for a Russian family that pays her "a little more" than minimum wage but treats her well. "Most people want to stay in Hong Kong, most of the domestic workers, if employers would help them," she says. "Sometimes it is hard. Hong Kong is full of regulations. Sometimes families are not easy to get along with. (Expenses) are more than domestic workers earn. I'm lucky. Some of my friends, their employers are not good to them." [7]

Carnate is one of more than 300,000 foreign domestic workers in Hong Kong. Half of them, like her, are from The Philippines, and they're nearly all female. Others come from Indonesia, Sri Lanka, India. Hong Kong laws require them to live with their employer—a law intended to keep them from taking second jobs and thus competing with local workers—and also prohibit them from every becoming permanent residents and thus eligible for state-run health care services and other benefits. Hong Kong's Court of Final Appeals ruled in March 2013 that foreign domestic workers don't qualify as "ordinary residents" and thus can't apply for permanent residence after seven years like other foreign workers in the city can.

Migrant workers – 200 million (crossing national borders) worldwide, including 40 million who are undocumented – are an essential part of the neoliberal global economic model pushed by the industrialized countries that make up the World Trade Organization as well as the World Bank and the International Monetary Fund, a model that promotes free trade and investment across national borders yet holds many workers in what the Southern Poverty Law Center calls "indentured servitude" or even slavery. The old ideologies of communism and Adam Smithian capitalism have little to do with this model and the global reach and power of its giant mega-corporations. Witness China, ostensibly a communist country yet a major player in the world of neoliberalism.

"Migrants are now a vital part of the service industry workforce in most developed countries," writes labor journalist David Bacon in his book *Illegal People*. "But migrant labor doesn't remain at the fringe of the economy. The world's oil industry is completely dependent on it. ... Employers gain great advantages from this system, particularly lower labor costs and increased workforce flexibility." [8]

Yet employers try to evade responsibility for the abuses in the system. "Its employment system is based on the use of contractors, which is replacing the system in which workers were directly employed by the businesses using their labor," Bacon writes. "Contract labor offers important advantages to employers. (They) have less and less responsibility for the actual conditions of employment or what happens to workers when work ends." [9]

When 112 workers died in the fire at the Tazreen garment factory in Dhaka, Bangladesh, in November 2012—the building had no fire exits--Walmart was quick to distance itself from the tragedy. Spokesmen said the retail giant had ended prior relations with the factory. Yet post-fire reports showed a third of the factory's production lines were committed to Walmart, and suppliers had used it that year. Five months later, on April 24, 2013, the eight-story Rana Plaza garment factory building in Savar, Bangladesh, collapsed, killing more than 1,100 people and injuring

2,500. Huge cracks had appeared in the building the day before, yet managers ordered workers back on the job. Walmart was a customer of a Rana Plaza factory.

Global corporations use "neoliberal reforms and economic treaties to displace communities, to produce a global army of available and vulnerable workers," Bacon writes. It's a worldwide problem that "nothing ... short of a radical reordering of the world's economy can fix." [10]

A 2014 report by the *New York Times* revealed at the United States spends $1.5 billion a year to buy uniforms and other clothing from Asian factories, many of them the same sweatshops built after the collapse of the textile industry in the U.S. South. Expect more with the approval of the Trans-Pacific Partnership, another NAFTA-like agreement that includes countries stretching from Canada and the United States to Vietnam, Brunei, Malaysia, and Singapore.

In shining, skyscraper-dominated Singapore – a city of five million where more than one-third of the workforce is foreign-born – many of the migrant workers live in crowded, rat-infested dormitories with little relief from the sweltering tropical heat, reliving the conditions that faced the 19th century immigrants from China who largely built Singapore.

The Rev. Carlton Eversley of Winston-Salem, North Carolina, an African-American activist who sees immigrant rights as a civil rights issue, says he will never forget the migrant labor camp he and other religious leaders visited in Wilson, N.C., in late 2009. "It was mind-boggling, 125 guys in wooden barracks, seven guys in a room with no windows, no ventilation, no linen, no bed sheets, no closets, very hot, very unsanitary, swarms of gnats. ... You felt like you were leaving the United States and going to some kind of Third World situation." [11]

Inherent in the global economy is the deep poverty and joblessness in the labor-exporting countries. Although overall poverty rates in Vietnam have been on the decline, one in three in the rural areas remains poor, like half the population of Mexico and two-thirds of the people in El Salvador, Honduras, and Nicaragua. Forty percent of the population in all Latin America is poor. In the Philippines, the country of origin for 70,000 workers in Taiwan, 44 percent of the population lives on less than $2 a day.

"The time has come to think about labor migration from a global labor solidarity perspective," writes Jennifer Gordon in *New Labor Forum*. Gordon calls for a Transnational Labor Citizenship that would be the core of a new legal framework requiring basic standards in the treatment of low-wage migrant workers. [12]

Taiwan's MENT, which includes the Taiwan International Workers Association as well as the VMWBO and other groups, has seen significant victories in recent years. In 2009, the Taiwanese government enacted a Human Trafficking Prevention & Control Law specifically geared to stop the kinds of abuses Nguyen's office handles. Enforcing the law and giving it more teeth are the next hurdles MENT faces.

MENT and its member organizations keep constant pressure on the government to put an end to sweatshop conditions--12-hours-a-day, seven-days-a-week jobs without breaks--and other abuses that can lead to death, whether in the factory or in cases such as that of 30-year-old engineer Hsieh Ming-hung who is believed to have died from overwork at Taiwan's HTC Corp in 2011. One of the top five smart phone makers in the world, HTC is led by Taiwan's richest person, Cher Wang. Such incidents and MENT pressure led the government's Council of Labor of Affairs to create clinics at nine major hospitals to treat overworked employees and to promise that employers will face criminal charges for work-hour violations.

MENT and others are also pushing to get more regulation to protect the nation's 160,000 foreign domestic workers, largely migrants from the Philippines, Vietnam, and other Asian countries. "If you are a caregiver, you work very long hours," says Nelva Baldon, a 32-year-old caregiver and activist from the city of Iloilo in the Philippines. "The government needs to do more. We don't have the laws protecting us. If we're sick, we have nothing. …The employers treat us like slaves. We understand we are workers, and we have to work but they treat us like slaves." [13]

"We need a little confrontation sometimes," agrees fellow caregiver Sheila Z. Mayanoia, 39, also from Iloilo. [14]

Filipino workers like Baldon and Mayanoia are important to the cause for workers rights in Taiwan, says Sister Eulalia P. Loreto of the Migrant Workers' Concern Desk at St. Christopher Catholic Church in Taipei. "Filipinos think they have to be heard.

They are vocal, and they insist on their rights." [15] The same is true in Hong Kong, says Cynthia Ca Abdon-Tellez, a native of The Philippines and general manager of the Mission for Migrant Workers in Hong Kong. "They (Filipinas) speak up. They're more organized." [16] Still, she says, workers from Indonesia, Bangladesh, and other countries are becoming increasingly vocal about their rights.

In faraway Sanford, N.C., where Diego Reyes Jr. and FLOC fight everyday for the rights of his father and other workers in North Carolina's tobacco and vegetable fields, the same issues exist. "Having some progress depends on laws and enforcement of laws," Reyes Jr. says. "There are very few that protect workers here. Farm workers are not covered by labor laws. Housing requirements are very poor." [17]

This is why Ohio-based FLOC has been fighting in North Carolina and other states for years to get growers and their corporate bosses to pay workers a just wage and provide reasonable working and living conditions. After a five-year campaign that included a JPMorgan Chase divestment effort to force the Wall Street powerhouse to intervene, the Reynolds American tobacco company finally agreed in the summer of 2012 to meet with FLOC regarding the health and work condition concerns of the 30,000 workers – most of them migrants – who work on tobacco farms in North Carolina and beyond. JPMorgan Chase leads a consortium of lenders that funnels close to $500 million in credit to Reynolds American.

"We want Reynolds to understand... they have the power and the money to influence the system," Reyes Jr. said. "We need Reynolds to understand they have a lot of responsibility." [18]

Statistics from FLOC and the National Farm Worker Ministry estimate that 24 percent of tobacco pickers suffer from nicotine poisoning each season. This along with exposure to harmful pesticides and long hours under the summer sun has led to strokes and even deaths. A greater consciousness of tobacco companies' responsibilities would have worldwide implications. In Kazakhstan, for example, migrant workers from surrounding countries harvest fields owned by Philip Morris International under similar conditions.

The JPMorgan Chase divestment campaign was similar to tactics that FLOC previously used successfully to organize migrant workers and insist on social justice for them. FLOC won agreements with the Campbell, Vlasic, Heinz and Dean Foods companies in the 1980s and 1990s and a landmark victory with the North Carolina-based Mt. Olive Pickle Company in 2004, the largest labor agreement in the U.S. South.

FLOC's charismatic founder and leader, Baldemar Velasquez, an evangelical minister and winner of the 1990 MacArthur Fellows Award, told *Southern Exposure* magazine once that his and others' efforts to improve the lot of migrant workers is part of a larger social movement, "a new Latino labor force all over the South that will be the foundation of the next civil rights movement in the U.S. – a movement that is going to have a brown face." [19]

FLOC is one of several organizing groups that have experienced success in recent years in the historically union-hostile U.S. South, a region more key than ever to the future of the U.S. labor movement. Workers at the Smithfield hog plant in Tar Heel, N.C., scored a major victory against a formidable anti-union management in 2009 when they gained a contract with the United Food and Commercial Workers. In September 2010, hundreds of mostly black, strike-ready workers – also members of the UFCW – at Delta Pride Catfish Inc. in the Mississippi Delta forced the company to go back to the bargaining table with a contract offer that restored wages and benefits it had sought to cut or eliminate.

Another organization in Mississippi, the Mississippi Immigrants Rights Alliance, has established itself as one of the region's foremost champions of worker rights, forging an alliance with the state Legislature's Black Caucus to kill Arizona-style anti-immigrant bills while helping to restore tens of thousands of dollars in back pay to migrant workers on the Gulf Coast.

The Coalition of Immokalee Workers (CIW) in Florida has waged campaigns similar to FLOC's Reynolds American campaign, most recently in its effort to get the state's largest grocery company, Publix, to pay growers a penny more for each pound of tomatoes Publix buys. The goal is to improve the lot of the industry's largely migrant workforce. The CIW has won similar agreements with Whole Foods, Burger King, McDonalds, Subway, and Yum Brands (which owns Taco Bell).

The CIW has also been active in exposing slavery-like conditions among migrant workers in Florida, leading to federal convictions and the imprisonment of several contractors and labor camp operators. "Slavery has taken on different forms today," writes Silvia Giagnoni in her book on the CIW, *Fields of Resistance*. "Unlike the system of chattel slavery in the United States, modern-day slavery is no longer a matter of ownership of people... but of total control over people's lives. ... Many times there are no chains or locked doors, only isolated places in the middle of the fields where alienated human beings live under the constant threat of beatings. The privation of individual liberty is deployed with the primary objective of obtaining profit." [20]

Slaves annually contribute some $13 billion to the global economy, according to Kevin Bales, author of *Disposable People: New Slavery in the Global Economy*.

Groups like FLOC and the CIW are building on the foundation of earlier efforts, such as the Southern Faith, Labor and Community Alliance's successful campaign to win a fair contract for workers with K-Mart in North Carolina in the mid-1990s. Another was the corporate campaign that won an agreement with the Duke Power Company in the 1970s to better the lot of miners at its union-busting Eastover mining company in Harlan County, Ky. The Institute for Southern Studies, a progressive media and research organization based in Durham, N.C., played a prominent role in that campaign.

An even earlier precedent was set by the Southern Tenant Farmers' Union, a biracial organization of more than 30,000 tenant farmers and sharecroppers in the Deep South that won agreements with several landlords against overwhelming odds in the 1930s.

"It's really an exciting time," says Alexandria Jones, a Winston-Salem, N.C.-based community organizer with the National Farm Workers Ministry, which has worked closely with FLOC in the Reynolds American campaign. "You have to go to the top to effect real economic change.

"There are a lot of amazing things going on," she told me during an interview in Winston-Salem. "In a lot of ways, the labor movement is strong. You have these smaller groups out there, groups of strong people, in areas of the greatest need, these people are working hard to make changes." [21]

These "amazing things" are going on across the Global South. Strikes at foreign-owned plants in India and China have showed that workers can achieve better wages and conditions when they stand together. Foxconn Technology and Honda, for example, responded by raising wages at their plants in China. Foxconn, with a workforce of more than 1 million Chinese, agreed in February 2013 to allow workers to elect their own union leaders, a break from the tradition of Communist Party officials picking plant managers to be union leaders.

This labor activism is moving beyond traditional labor unionism in raising worker consciousness and forcing governments and corporations to pay attention.

An example is the Asia Floor Wage Alliance, a grassroots movement founded in India in October 2009 to promote a pan-Asia minimum wage for low-paid garment workers. An estimated 54 percent of the world's clothes are made in Asia. The AFW now boasts member organizations in 11 Asian nations as well as member trade unions and other labor advocacy groups in Europe and North America.

"Capital movement has gone beyond the borders of state regulation, savagely moving in and out countries while searching for cheaper production costs and ever more relaxed labor environments," writes Rita Olivia Tambunan, executive secretary of the Trade Union Rights Centre in Jakarta, in *International Union Rights* magazine. "The organizational power of unions has been weakened by the flexibilization of labor. While most of them are still struggling to build union capacity, the oppressive anti-union policy also hampers unions in Asian countries."

The Asia Floor Wage Alliance is "an effort to depart from this situation," she writes. [22]

The AFW is one of many examples of the "global labor solidarity" that Jennifer Gordon seeks. FLOC, the United Farm Workers, United Auto Workers, the United Steel Workers Union, and especially the United Electrical, Radio & Machine Workers of America (UE) have worked across borders with unions in Mexico, Canada and beyond. The Alliance of Progressive Workers (APL) in the Philippines has helped organize workers in Hong Kong. Trade unions in Nepal and Korea have worked closely together in helping Nepalese migrant workers in Korea.

Bringing attention to these global efforts are publications and Internet magazines and news services like *International Union Rights, LabourStart, Global Voices, Portside*, and, in the U.S. South, *Facing South*, the flagship online publication of the Institute for Southern Studies. These media organizations fill the yawning chasm of missing coverage left by national and international mainstream media, and they tell the stories of the voiceless millions who otherwise toil namelessly in the global economy.

Of course, the odds are formidable against these labor alliances. Social movements always face what seem to be impossible odds. Witness the Civil Rights Movement in the United States, the Solidarity movement in Poland. The power of global corporations and the government and mainstream media organizations that promote and support them cannot be overestimated. However, when the lowest paid workers in the U.S. South – tobacco pickers, cucumber pickers, and catfish plant workers – can stand up to their bosses and force agreements that meet their demands, when groups representing lowly migrant workers in Taiwan and Singapore can make government take action on their behalf, something is afoot in this global economy, and it doesn't take a Mahatma Gandhi or a Martin Luther King Jr. to know what it is.

Alexandria Jones, a community organizer with the National Farm Workers Ministry in Winston-Salem, North Carolina, USA. *Photo credit: Joseph B. Atkins.*

NORTH AND CENTRAL AMERICA

CHAPTER ONE

"Workers aren't a disposable product. They are the sole reason why everyone in this country has food on their table."

The Story of Eulogio Solanoa

As told to author-photographer David Bacon

Eulogio Solanoa is a Mixteco migrant from Oaxaca, and was a farm worker for many years. After leading strikes and community protests, he went to work as an organizer for the United Farm Workers. Today he lives in Greenfield, California, where he told his story to David Bacon. Thanks to Farmworker Justice for the support for this project of documenting the lives of farm workers.

I've been here in Greenfield since 1992, so that's twenty years. But I'm from a small town called San Jose de las Flores in the Putla district in Oaxaca. My family has ejido land there -- not a lot of land, just what they call a cajon, less than a quarter of an acre. That's about the amount of land everyone has there. We only have enough to live, but not enough to buy a house or car. My father didn't even own any land -- the land we have comes from my mother.

The entire town is an ejido [communities created by Mexico's land reform that hold their land in common], but everyone has their own little piece of land. We don't choose a different plot each year -- whatever piece of land you first got is what you keep. That is what Emiliano Zapata fought for, so that everyone can have their own land. We didn't have that before. But it's not enough land for a family to live, only enough to grow corn and a few beans. It's enough to eat, but not enough to grow crops to sell.

That's why we didn't have clothes and barely enough to eat. When I was fourteen and going to school I still didn't own a pair of shoes. I was barefoot. I really enjoyed going to school, though. My teacher said I was the brightest one in class. But I couldn't continue - I had to go to work with my family.

At first folks from my hometown would leave to work in Morelos, where they'd pick tomatoes. Then gradually people went to work in construction in Guerrero and Acapulco. Little by little they began to travel further north, to Sinaloa, Sonora and Baja California. When I heard that some relatives were going to cross the border to the U.S., I decided to go with them. I'd heard that money was so plentiful here you could literally sweep it off the floor. When I got here, though, I realized things were not as I was told.

I was twenty - the first in my family to leave. My entire world had been confined to our small town. My parents didn't want to let me come to the United States, but since I was old enough, it was my decision. When I crossed the border and started sending them money, their attitude changed. In those years nobody had a cell phone, so communicating with them was difficult - by letter. To send money to them I had to use the telegraph or money orders. I worked for a while and then returned home. When I decided to come north a second time, they didn't worry as much. They knew I was coming here to work. My mother passed away sixteen years ago, but my father still lives in Oaxaca. I've been sending money back this whole time because people don't have anything back home.

The dollar is the only thing that counts in Mexico. If I work ten hours a day here, I earn $80. If I were to work that same amount of time in Mexico, the most I could hope to earn is 200 pesos -- about $16. That's a big difference, especially when you take into account the price of food. A kilo of meat in Mexico costs 120 pesos. You don't even earn enough to eat in Mexico. Here you do. Because I had a job I could pay my rent, buy food and even have a car. I know I'm not going to get rich, but I have had a better life here. If you take the money you earn here with you to Mexico, it's a substantial amount to people there.

When I first got here I was afraid because people said gringos ate people like us up. Well, there is some truth to that. They do eat us alive, but not in the way I first thought. They eat us alive in the sense that we leave our lives out in the fields. We come here to work in the fields at the age of 20 or 22 and by the time we're 45, we can no longer do that work anymore. It's a very difficult job, starting at four in the morning until sun down. Fifty-year-old men have already spent their lives out in the fields, and then they can't find work there anymore. That's why indigenous people think the gringos eat us alive. They do.

I crossed the border the first time in 1990, with a friend, and we went to San Diego. We lived under trees. In Carlsbad we build a shack out of cardboard we'd collected. We cooked with firewood and bathed in the river in freezing water. That's how we saved money. I wasn't even familiar with U.S. coins. I would go and buy something at the store and simply take out my coins for the cashier to take. They probably took more than I owed, but I had this blind faith that people here weren't like in Mexico and weren't going to rob me blind.

We lived under the trees there for three months. Then we headed to Madera, where I picked peppers and tomatoes. Then I picked strawberries in Santa Maria. In Santa Maria many immigrants are from Sinaloa and Guanajuato. They're tall and fair, and they made fun of us for being short and dark. It made me mad when they'd call us Oaxacos or Oaxaquitos, because I'm Mexican just like them. We don't call them Michoacanitos or Guanajuatitos. The people that call us those names think we're inferior. But we respect others regardless of what Mexican state they're from, and ask for that same respect back.

In Santa Maria I learned to speak Spanish. In my home town, we didn't speak Spanish, just Mixteco. The only person that spoke Spanish was the schoolteacher. It makes me think of the many places here in California where teachers speak English and all the students speak Spanish. That's the way it was for us, growing up speaking Mixteco. In Mexico people made fun of us indigenous kids because we couldn't speak Spanish properly. I knew just a little Spanish before I came. As soon as I got here I began to attend community meetings to learn Spanish and understand this country's laws. This was a foreign country to me then, and I wanted to learn more. I eventually learned Spanish and became familiar with this country's laws so that I would know how to defend myself.

The foremen in the strawberries quickly learned that indigenous people from Guerrero, Oaxaca and Chiapas had already worked on farms back home, and found we were very good workers. They began to hire more of us. But they wanted us to work really fast, as if we were disposable and made of rubber. Finally I moved to Greenfield from Santa Maria, because they paid more here.

All the jobs I've done have been hard, but a lot depends on the foreman. I once worked for a foreman who herded his workers as if we were animals. I didn't like that. Another foreman was very disrespectful. When one worker asked for a drink of water, after we hadn't had anything to drink for two hours, he grabbed his private parts and said that was the hose if he wanted water. But I've also worked for foremen who treated us well and knew we were just there to do our job. Some are good and some are bad.

Picking grapes is one of the worst jobs. Many workers get sick because of the sulfur on the vines. It makes your eyes and skin sting. My nose would become swollen and I wouldn't be able to work. Then you bring the chemical home on your clothes, and it hurts your family. Foremen would lure us to work in those fields by telling us they would pay us 25 cents more an hour. But when we got sick, they weren't responsible. Of course we had no health insurance either.

The hardest jobs I've had were picking peas and strawberries. Picking peas you work on your knees all day. It's a delicate crop, so you can't carry more than two or three pounds at a time. Your nails take the hardest hit when picking peas. They give you a sort of metal finger so that you can cut the pods off of the vine, but you still have to use your nail. Sometimes it splits in half.

It's the same when you pick strawberries. You can't really use your fingers. You have to use your nail because you can't squeeze the fruit. You also work bent over all day, and soon your back really starts to hurt. You work that way from sunrise to sundown for eight months of the year. After a few years you develop permanent back problems, and after you're 40 or 45 you can't do that work anymore.

People in packing plants work standing up, so you often see older workers there. Not in strawberry fields. People who work in offices work in cool conditions. In the fields we work in extreme heat and for longer hours. If you put each of your hands on something hot and cold, what burns faster? The hand over a hot surface. It's the same for those working under the sun. We burn out a lot faster.

The wages are not enough to support a family. Eight dollars an hour is very little. The price of food has gone up. Back when I was earning $6 or $7 an hour, the price of gas was $1.49 to $1.99. Now the price of gas is close to $5 a gallon. We don't earn much more than we used to, but the price of everything has skyrocketed. When the housing market went up, our rent went up a lot. About ten years ago, you could rent a two-bedroom home for $450 or $500. Now that has shot up to $1,000 a month. Our hourly wage was $7.50 and it hasn't doubled just because the price of housing doubled. If our wages were to keep up with the high cost of everything, we should be earning $14 to $15 right now. $8 an hour just isn't enough.

I don't understand why wages are so low. It seems as though the government isn't at all concerned with the minimum wage. I think it's probably because people don't speak up. But the unequal treatment of farm workers comes from the government. It's the government's job to make sure there is equality, and that farm workers are treated like other workers. But people working in restaurants or most other jobs receive overtime pay after eight hours. The law says you only have to pay farm workers overtime after ten hours instead. Of course farmers like this law, because it saves them money.

Wages are rising a little in this area because farmers can't attract enough workers to pick their crops. They need workers, and it's not uncommon to see lettuce and broccoli machines only half full of workers. Plus, there have been work stoppages throughout the years because workers are trying to raise wages.

I worked for one grower, Amaral, for ten years. Years before I got there the company had provided workers with work equipment like hats and shirts. To do the job you also have to have rubber boots, because the fields are so wet, and knives to cut the crop from the plant. But in 1999 the owner stopped supplying that equipment, telling workers they had to buy their own. In addition, he said we had to contribute a dollar to purchase water for the crew. The foreman literally held out a hat and everyone formed a line and dropped a dollar in the hat for water. We were treated very badly.

Finally, in 2001 a group of workers walked out when one worker cut himself and the foreman wouldn't report it. He told him to keep working, that he could easily go to the border and hire a new group of workers. But they didn't really protest. They just left, and got jobs at other companies that were paying more. Amaral's owner had been paying $6.50 an hour, and had to give workers a 50-cent raise.

Three years later, Amaral workers went on strike again, asking for higher wages. The owner promised to begin giving us equipment again, and to give us a 35-cent raise. But it was all talk. In the end he didn't give us anything. Workers went on strike again in 2007. The UFW [United Farm Workers Union] came in, wanting to represent the workers. The workers weren't interested, though, and said they'd handle the situation on their own. They believed the owner would do the right thing and meet their demands. While union representatives were there, a truck full of work equipment pulled up and the company handed it out. But that was it. There was no increase or any improvements after that.

Another three years passed with no change. Foremen continued to mistreat workers. They paid them for ten hours when they'd actually work eleven or twelve. Workers were even asked to start fifteen to thirty minutes before the official start time and weren't paid for that either. They had no water, and had to purchase supplies on their own. So they decided to strike again last year. The UFW asked the workers if they wanted the union to represent them and were once again were sent away. The owner brought in work equipment, and the workers once again fell for it.

This year the workers finally asked the UFW to represent them. The union was skeptical, and said they'd only represent the workers if a majority were for it. They made the owner sign a written contract because he had promised so much earlier and not delivered.

I supported the strikes, but at first another worker led them. He didn't do a good job. When they planned their work stoppage, and all of the workers respected the action and stayed home, he actually went to work. The workers were so angry with him they almost beat him. Later I led the effort with other workers. There were many indigenous workers and I translated when they communicated with the foreman, so he accused me of being the instigator. But I liked helping in that way. That's when I began to work with the union, participating in the marches and meetings.

Then the union invited me to work for them. Because it was winter, I wasn't working in the fields, so I decided to take the job. I worked for them for three and a half years, and just recently went back to work for them again. The UFW recently signed a contract with D'Arrigo Brothers Produce, and assigned me to work with workers in the mustard and lettuce departments. Before that I worked with broccoli workers.

We're currently working with workers in non-union companies too. They have real bargaining power right now because the growers need workers. It's a good time to ask for family health insurance benefits, holiday pay, bonuses and fair treatment. Cesar Chavez fought for all of those things. All workers deserve those benefits. Workers aren't a disposable product. They are the sole reason why everyone in this country has food on their table.

I think the union saw all I did for my community on a voluntary basis. My previous work and service spoke for me. I didn't ask them for a job. It was God's will to put me in their path. Over the years the union has hired people who speak indigenous languages, and that's where I fit in. When they couldn't communicate with some workers, they brought me in to help. There are many workers who don't speak Spanish well, and they're abused because of it. I think the union discovered that problem.

That is part of the reason for the injustices we faced in Greenfield. Many people from Mexico, Central and South America come here without knowing anything about this country. They come from places where they didn't even own a mule and have certainly never owned a vehicle. People arriving here live even eight or ten to a house. Folks around here aren't used to seeing that. I think that's where the problem started.

We came here to work, and we're residents of this community. We spend our dollars here Many long time residents do their shopping in Paso Robles and surrounding cities, but we shop locally. If you look around at local stores and laundromats, all you see are Oaxaqueños. But immigration raids began and they arrested 27 Triquis. We began holding informational meetings, but the city police began to hound Triquis, Oaxaqueños and anyone indigenous. They would arrest them and impound their vehicles. So we began to work with the police department, to teach them about where we come from, about our people and culture. We met with city council officials, and many non-profit and government agencies, asking for justice and trying to educate them.

In 2001, the city council passed a resolution that said immigration officials could only come into town if they had a list of criminals they were looking for. But some residents began trying to repeal it. Many of us fought back and 700 people protested with the support of the UFW in front of City Hall, asking for an end to racism. We also celebrated Cesar Chavez's anniversary in a large public celebration.

In 2003 the indigenous people living in Greenfield held a meeting and hosted a celebration in appreciation of the information that had been shared with them, thanking the police department, city leaders, state representatives, school officials and mainly the UFW. The UFW president, Arturo Rodriguez, and Dolores Huerta came.

We started holding monthly meetings to inform residents of what is and isn't allowed in this city, county and country. People who didn't like them called them the Oaxaca meetings, but any resident could attend. The Chief of Police was simply providing information to whoever wanted to hear it, about driver's education and local laws. That's when some longtime Greenfield residents got angry. They eventually fired the Chief of Police with a ridiculous excuse -- that he had once appeared on a Spanish television news show without asking his supervisor for permission.

In reality he was fired because of racism toward the indigenous community. Farm workers came out to defend him and protested. But there was political division among the city leaders. Some listened to those longtime residents and they won. I'm not a citizen yet, but I know that was an injustice.

I'm proud I've served my community. I really enjoy what I do and I've learned a great deal, especially working for the union. I have five children, and my wife and I make seven. My oldest son is eighteen and my youngest daughter is two. I know they will speak three languages -- Mixteco, English and Spanish. They are learning a great deal and I see a bright future for them here. Speaking three languages will allow them to communicate with many people. They're great kids and I hope they find good jobs. I think they'll always live in the U.S., because this is their home, but if they want to visit or live in Mexico, that's their decision.

We eat our traditional Mixteco meals. The meat here has many chemicals, so we try and stay true to our Mixteco diet because it's healthier. If we ate American food, we would be obese in three months. We stick to eating mole and chakatan and quelite, which is a plant. There are some that make fun of us and say we're cheap and prefer to only eat plants. They think we're stupid, but in fact it's a healthier option than hamburgers and pizza.

As long as I'm alive they'll continue to stay connected to our culture. We still speak Mixteco. Even the youngest can speak it. I would love for them to speak as many languages as possible. Whether my grandchildren will also speak Mixteco will depend on them, but as long as I live, I'll continue to insist they learn our language. It's a gift from God and as our vows says, "What God has made, let man not separate." It's the same thing with our culture. Man should not take away the gift that God gave us.

Mariane Carnate, a native of The Philippines and domestic worker in Hong Kong. *Photo credit: Joseph B. Atkins.*

CHAPTER TWO

The Coalition of Immokalee Workers: Grassroots Politics in the Age of Corporate Media [1]

By

Silvia Giagnoni

Associate Professor, Department of Communication and Theatre
Auburn University, Montgomery, Alabama, USA

The fulcrum of the southwest Florida town of Immokalee is a dusty parking lot called by the old residents "The Pantry" after the *tienda* located there. This is Immokalee's labor pool, the place where farm workers gather early in the morning to secure their seats on one of the school buses that will take them to the often-faraway fields surrounding the town. The pickers, mostly immigrants, travel for hours to reach their workplace; they travel in the pitch dark of the night, midday, at dusk, and when the sun rises out east, because they never know what the crew leader or the weather or else has in store for them any given day in these forgotten lands. This is the life of a farmworker in 21st century America.

But it only takes a short walk from "The Pantry" for the women and men who work the fields of southwest Florida and beyond to find community. And hope. Here are located the colorful offices of the Coalition of Immokalee Workers.

***

This short essay intends to celebrate the CIW's winning recipe for social change. Thanks to the CIW, change is underway in Florida's agricultural industry. In these anti-union, corporate times, the CIW offers an example of steady, positive progress in the struggle for fairness and justice for the migrants. It is a beacon of hope for other grassroots, worker-led movements all over the globe. Back in 2007, it made me, then a disillusioned graduate student from Italy, believe, once again, in "doing politics," which is what democracy is about: people having the power to affect social change.

The CIW's Fair Food Program represents today a major labor achievement in an industry infamously implicated, even most recently, in modern-day slavery cases. Between 1997 and 2010, the FBI, with the invaluable help of the CIW, uncovered eight cases involving over 1,200 workers in Florida and elsewhere in the Southeast. [2]

Chief Assistant U.S. Attorney Douglas Molloy called the Florida fields "ground zero" for modern-day slavery in the United States. And where poor working and living conditions are found, the norm is exploitation. That's why the Coalition was first formed: to improve the conditions of the workers of Immokalee. And it has.

An increasing number of farms are now participating in the Fair Food Program, which on its website is described as "a unique partnership among farmers, farmworkers, and retail food companies that ensures human wages and working conditions for the workers who pick fruits and vegetables." [3]

Not only are the pickers paid fairer wages today, but the CIW-inspired Fair Food Standards Council is also monitoring their working conditions through regular audits and a 24-hour toll-free hotline; all workers receive information about their rights at the point of hire and are able to participate in face-to-face education sessions with CIW on the farm and on the clock. Abuses are now routinely being reported. When growers are not complying, there are consequences as the Fair Food agreements are legally binding. It truly is a new day in the fields of the Sunshine State. [4]

But how has the CIW been able to get to this point? What does it take to get Fortune Top 500 corporations to give in to the requests of a rather small worker organization located next to a dusty parking lot in a town with a weird-sounding name in the middle of the Florida fields?

How do you change an industry—the U.S. produce industry — whose many growers, especially in the Southeast, have never parted from an exploitative instrumental mentality in their relations with the workers? How do you raise awareness about workers' rights issues without the backing of corporate media?

***

First, you need to pick a just cause.

Before the Fair Food Program was thoroughly implemented in the Florida fields, [5] most tomato pickers working in the state received sub-poverty wages: to earn a minimum wage a farmworker needed to pick 2.5 tons of tomatoes and work 10 hours a day. Women routinely experienced sexual harassment in the fields and rarely reported such abuses for fear of retaliation. Workers weren't allowed to have water breaks or to rest in the shade.

All too often, this is the reality of the over 200 million migrant workers estimated to exist in the world: a reality of exploitation. Migrant labor is made up of "an army of vulnerable workers," as David Bacon puts it. The cause of the migrants is a just one, but a key element in the CIW's winning tactic to improve workplace treatment has been the framing of the issue. Every once in a while, critics have brought up the fact that "illegals" are working in agriculture and that the CIW should not represent "those people," as if bringing up the citizenship status of some of the migrants could actually change the reality of exploitation. That only diverts attention from the real issue. Corporate buyers have used the "labor dispute" argument, claiming that what was going on "out there in the fields" was none of their business. The CIW's response has been, in a nutshell: this is about basic human rights. It's not about immigration, and it's really not about labor either. Simple and effective. Yet, how do you mobilize consumers?

Second, you start small.

So far, the CIW has focused its campaigns on just one of the crops harvested in Florida, though an important one. In the wintertime, 90 percent of the tomatoes consumed in the United States come from the Sunshine State. Rather than targeting the farmers, the Coalition decided to call to task the corporations who buy the produce.

When the organization was first formed, CIW members attempted to have a dialogue with the growers. For a few years, farmers and local legislators were the chief targets of the CIW actions. In 1997, after a 30-day hunger strike by six CIW members, one grower said: "The tractor doesn't tell the farmer how to run the farm."

Despite such displays of arrogance, the movement kept growing and soon expanded beyond Florida: it relied on creating a solidarity network like no other and on the resilience of the CIW members. In 2000, this initial tactic culminated with the two-week-long, 230-mile march from Immokalee to the Orlando headquarters of the Florida Fruit and Vegetable Association, the powerful lobbying arm of the state's agricultural industry. That raised awareness around the issue locally, but it didn't help much with changing an archaic and exploitative system.

Farmworkers have been historically paid by piece rate, not hourly, so their wages depend on how much produce they pick and, ultimately, on how good the harvest is. The Coalition then figured out that it would ask corporations to pay one penny per pound more (*un centavo mas*) for the tomatoes workers picked. Such a small-yet-symbolic amount would effectively contrast with the millions of dollars of profit that the corporations made.

Farmworkers are excluded by most workplace protections and the collective bargaining provisions of the National Labor Relations Act of 1935 and by most of the provisions of the Fair Labor Standard Acts of 1938. This is a workforce that legally has no right to organize. However, the lack of a federal law allowed agricultural workers to bring forward their requests to a third party. And so did the CIW, reaching an agreement with Taco Bell first (and, specifically, with its owner, Yum Brands), and McDonald's afterward, plus all the other buyers that have followed suit: Burger King (2008), Whole Foods Market (2008), Aramark (2010), Sodexo (2010), Trader Joe's (2012), Walmart (2014) and Fresh Market (2015), among others. [6] The fight was similar to that of Cesar Chávez and his United Farm Workers, which had also carried out a secondary boycott against grocery chains selling boycotted grapes and lettuce back in the 1970s.

The CIW turned a disadvantaged position—no right to unionize—into a tactic to further mobilize consumers; it made a virtue of necessity and capitalized on the increased freedom of action that the law allowed agricultural workers. Like in other migrant communities, the high turnover of the labor force renders the adoption of traditional forms of workers' organization practically impossible in Immokalee. Further, to bring attention to an isolated community that barely appears on the maps, the CIW needed allies: people elsewhere who worked hard to raise awareness and prompted a popular mobilization, a consumers' mobilization. Thus, the Student/Farmworker Alliance and Interfaith Action were created in the late 1990s and early 2000s, and the Campaign for Fair Food was soon born.

The CIW members and their allies knew that if they wanted to transform the food chain, if they wanted to promote accountability and create a model of social responsibility in the U.S. produce industry, in other words, if they wanted to change the system, they needed ultimately to target the corporations. They needed to put pressure at the top. In the end, it is the corporate buyers who demand the lowest possible prices from their suppliers (the farmers). And this pressure to keep the cost of labor low could have been lifted only if consumers became aware of the living and working conditions of the Immokalee workers.

Third, you go after the corporations' public image.

Consumers have incredible power. That power is economic democracy, today much more powerful, I'd argue, than electoral democracy: the idea of using your money as a tool to make change in the world. It's because of our buying choices that corporations make a profit. So how do you go about activating the general public and get consumers to act upon this pretty simple fact? Well, you begin by exposing the modern-day slavery conditions behind the tomatoes you may find at the store; you foreground the workers, the human beings who pick your produce. This way, you change the conversation; you change public discourse around food and consumerism. We are part of a global community whose members are reciprocally related economically, and thus socially and culturally. Geographical distance may alienate us from the producers, so we shouldn't underestimate the benefits of changing the conversation in the Global North to trigger a positive cycle of change. The exploitation occurs close to home, not in the Global South, but on U.S. soil: in the 21st century, modern-day slavery happens next door, and we shouldn't turn a blind eye to it. The Coalition has sent its members all over the country to speak to church groups, schools, and a variety of communities to increase awareness about what they do. A typical scenario:

Who wants to try and lift this bucket of tomatoes? The farmworker prompts the audience. She stands by a red bushel of dry rice: she is really not much taller than the bucket, and her indigenous features betray her Central American origins. A white guy in his mid-twenties, a member of Interfaith Action, is standing next to her and helps with the translation. The bucket weighs 32 pounds when full, she says, while a couple of volunteers from the audience approach the bushel. The Immokalee workers must carry it to a truck parked at the edge of a field. With the bucket on their shoulders, they walk to the truck. Then they throw it up in the air to a man on the truck who empties it. They earn 50 cents for picking and carrying 32 pounds of tomatoes. They do this up to 50 times a day.

***

Fourth, you highlight the corporations' contradictions.

The CIW demands buyers to add one penny per pound to the cost of their tomatoes. It is a small amount that makes a big difference in the wages of the workers. In 2006, Burger King recorded $2.23 billion in profit. Yet, for months Burger King staunchly refused to accept the CIW conditions that would cost the company a fraction of that amount. In *Fields of Resistance* (2011), I recount one incident that precipitated the signing of the agreement with Burger King in May 2008. [7] High-ranked personnel of the corporation used pseudonyms and, in the case of then-BK Vice President Steve Grover, his own daughter's handle, to post defamatory videos on the web. BK hired an unlicensed private investigation company specializing in the infiltration of unions and other grassroots groups to spy on the future actions and workings of the CIW. This "BK-gate" was uncovered just a few weeks before the Burger King and CIW joint announcement.

At the time of writing (February 2015), Publix is still buying tomatoes from non-participating growers—that 10 percent of farmers who are not part of the FTGE. The Southeastern grocery store chain has in fact yet to sign an agreement with the CIW. Publix has yet an entire line of organic, environmentally friendly products called Greenwise Market. It also sells its own fair trade coffee. Its label reads: "Fair trade prices help small farmers provide employees with livable wages and work conditions. Which fosters the same values we do: community, well-being, and a nicer world."

How does this same company reconcile selling fair trade products that support workers in the Global South by paying them fair wages while turning a blind eye to CIW requests and allowing exploitation in Florida's fields to continue? The penny per pound is a premium, yet the Florida-based company refused to do the right thing "at home." Exposing such contradictions is a key step in putting pressure on corporate buyers.

"If there are some atrocities going on, it's not our business," Publix spokesperson Dwaine Stevens has said. "Maybe it's something the government should get involved with."

Whenever Publix the retailer has tried to convey the message that it is not accountable for what happens in the fields, the CIW has forced consumers to connect the dots and see how this company, too, actually is.

In 2011, Publix released a "Put it in the Price" defense. "We are unaware of a single instance of slavery existing in our supply chain," the statement read. "Publix is also unaware of a single instance of payment of less than the required minimum wage."

Truth be told, farmworkers have been historically victims of wage theft. In pre – and post-harvest work, agricultural labor is actually paid hourly. This is not the case during the harvesting season: then, at the end of each pay period, a calculation should be performed to ensure that a farmworker's gross earnings are in compliance with the minimum wage. If they are not, employers should add the adjustment to the worker's check.

In reality, such a scenario was the exception, not the norm, before the CIW established a code of conduct and struck a deal with the farmers. Now, growers who participate in the Fair Food Program are required to have an electronic timekeeping system that helps monitors make sure there's a record of the hours tomato pickers actually work as well as a matching fair pay.

Fifth, you do it creatively.

The CIW has embraced the tradition of nonviolent protest of the civil rights movement; the Fair Food movement speaks often in spiritual, if not overtly, religious terms, and references to Christian symbolism are an integral part of the struggle: for instance, the breaking of the bread that took place at the end of a seven-day fast in front of the Publix headquarters in Lakeland, Florida, in March 2012. Quotes from the Bible are often used to reinforce and illustrate important steps in the struggle or the just cause farmworkers are fighting. The input of many churches and religious organizations—not only Christian but also Jewish and Buddhist—has given the movement for fair food a highly spiritual character to say the least. The fact that the heart of the struggle is in the Southeast, arguably the most religious area of the country, has definitely added to that imprint.

In addition, the CIW has used the charismatic power of musicians, such as Zack de La Rocha and guitarist Tom Morello of Rage Against the Machine, and the influential support of the Kennedy family to its own advantage. Food writers such as Raj Patel, Tom Philpott and Eric Schlosser as well as *The Nation*'s editor and publisher Katrina Van Heuvel have written in support of the CIW's struggles and the Fair Food Program. The Fair Food movement has grown thanks to the creative forces that have intellectually and artistically supported it all throughout the years.

In particular, numerous artists have lent their talents to create colorful memories (signs, photos, videos or other artwork) and have spread them all over social media: one of these is Philadelphia-based photographer JJ Tizou who used crowdsourcing as a way to support his project and asked CIW allies to support his trip to Florida to photograph the March for Rights, Respect & Fair Food in March 2013. Author, artist puppeteer and antiwar organizer David Solnit has helped CIW members and their allies dramatize their struggles and achievements as well as modern-day slavery cases. In addition to these re-enactments, colorful, wooden signs and flags and even papier-mâché statues have been the trademark of CIW campaigns.

To further reach people and raise awareness of past and current farmworkers' conditions, CIW members travelled with their Florida Modern-Day Slavery Museum all over the United States between 2010 and 2011. The exhibits were mostly hosted in a large cargo container, a replica of the one used to keep workers captive overnight in a recently uncovered slavery operation. The museum tours exposed thousands of people to the shocking contemporary reality of modern-day slavery, which leads me to my last point. You try to reach as many people as possible.

Sixth, you do it politically.

You do politics, the art of creating consensus among different people around issues and then act upon such a consensus.

The CIW understood early on that the focus of the farmworkers' struggle shouldn't be the composition of the Florida agricultural labor force—today primarily made up of immigrants from Mexico, Guatemala and Haiti—and thus the vulnerability of its many undocumented workers. Illegal immigration is a topic way too controversial, and it would attract undesirable attention to the community of Immokalee. To create consensus around such a complicated issue with its unjust-yet-invisible reality, the CIW understood it had to focus on the least controversial aspects of its struggle: human rights. This has been, to some extent, a rhetorical move, a necessary linguistic shift to aid the farmworkers in the building of a larger coalition of allies. Yet the harsh reality of the eight modern-day slavery cases uncovered in the Florida fields further proved to the world that the cause of the farmworkers in the Southeast "qualified" for the term as much as any other human rights cause in the Global South. Farm workers' poverty is a worker rights issue, one may argue; yet the CIW has mobilized the figure of the farmworker as one whose human rights (and not just labor rights) have been routinely abused. It worked.

If you are to create a large "rainbow" movement, as environmentalist and CIW supporter Oannes Pritzker called it, you need to create consensus around a just cause, start small and simple, deconstruct and expose those corporate messages that are meant to deny the reality of injustice. You need to re-conquer language and, with it, you may also reconquer politics. And you do it with a smile, colorfully.

Coalición! Presente!

Cynthia Ca Abdon-Tellez, general manager of the Mission for Migrant Workers in Hong Kong. *Photo credit: Joseph B. Atkins.*

EUROPE, NORTH AFRICA AND BEYOND

CHAPTER THREE

How LabourStart Campaigns Globally for Workers Rights

by

Eric Lee

Author and Founding Editor, *LabourStart*

London, England

LabourStart (www.labourstart.org) is a decentralized, informal network of hundreds of individuals around the world who collectively produce a website and news service that has become, in effect, the daily newspaper and campaigning platform of the international labour movement.

I founded *LabourStart* in March 1998, initially as a modest, one-man website that ran links to a few news stories every day. But after moving to London later that year, *LabourStart* opened up to volunteers to add news – and the network grew.

The news they have been adding comes from trade union websites, alternative news sources, and mainstream media. Where possible, correspondents are encouraged to look for what unions are saying about the news, to tell their side of the story.

The news links they post can be in any one of dozens of languages, including not only the world's major languages but some quite unusual ones. *LabourStart* has encouraged the translation of its interface and the recruitment of correspondents in every part of the world, and unlike most major international trade union websites, it doesn't restrict itself to the five or six major global languages.

They typically post about 250 news stories every day, or 90,000 every year, making *LabourStart* probably the largest repository of trade union news on the net.

LabourStart has also taken a different approach to how its news gets distributed, and many trade unionists will see *LabourStart's* news stories without ever visiting the *LabourStart* website. This is because from the very beginning *LabourStart* offered newswires free of charge to any trade union website that wanted one. Those newswires work in JavaScript and RSS, and over 300 union websites use them.

By 2015, *LabourStart* was also offering up apps designed for smartphones and tablets in both Android and iOS, allowing many people who don't even have access to desktop or laptop computers, particularly in developing countries, to read the news.

Finally, some of *LabourStart's* volunteer correspondents have made a point of posting top news stories throughout the day to *LabourStart's* popular Twitter feed and Facebook page.

***

In addition to collecting and disseminating news, *LabourStart* has from the very beginning served as a campaigning platform for trade unionists, and is now used by nearly all the global union federations (GUFs) for this purpose.

Global union federations are some of the oldest trade union institutions in the world. They unite national trade unions according to sector, so teachers' unions would affiliate to the Education International, journalists' unions would join the International Federation of Journalists, transport workers join the International Transport Workers Federation, and so on.

GUFs have been the main source of *LabourStart* campaigns for several years, though *LabourStart* also runs campaigns on behalf of the International Trade Union Confederation (ITUC), national trade union centers, national and local trade unions, and a number of non-governmental organizations.

Campaigns are proposed by GUFs or others, and consist of a headline, some background text explaining the issue, and a short default message to be sent to the target company or government.

They are translated in up to twenty languages and run for a maximum of three months.

LabourStart defines its campaigns as partnerships with the unions which have proposed them, and this is expressed by clearly labeling every campaign with the sponsoring union's name, logo and link to its website.

There is no point in launching an online campaign of any kind without publicity, and *LabourStart* has now had nearly two decades of experience in this field. The main way to publicize these campaigns is through email, primarily to *LabourStart's* dozens of language-based mailing lists. Those lists have grown tremendously over the years and by mid-2015 they included the email addresses of over 133,000 trade union activists in nearly every part of the world. Typically, one in ten of the people who receive a message will support a campaign, sometimes more and sometimes less.

In addition, *LabourStart* makes extensive use of social media to publicize its campaigns, primarily through Facebook and Twitter, but all the evidence points to email as being the most effective tool we have to build large campaigns.

But it's not the number of people who sign up to a campaign that matters. We don't define victory by numbers, but by results on the ground. If a union has asked us to help get one of its leaders released from jail, it doesn't matter if we send 10,000 messages or 20,000 messages – what matters in the end is, did we get the brother or sister released?

Do the campaigns work?

The short answer is: sometimes. As with any kind of campaigning activity we probably lose more often than we win. But when we win, we change peoples' lives.

Here are four examples from 2014:

* In the Philippines, a *LabourStart* campaign was crucial to a victory at NXP Semiconductors. Dismissed members of the union's executive were re-hired, big wage hikes were agreed with the employer, and many contractual workers were offered permanent, regular employment. An attempt by the employer to crush the union was resoundingly defeated.

* A *LabourStart* campaign called at the request of the German food workers union NGG contributed to a big win for the

workers at Autogrill in 2014. Following months of strike action and a large, sharp campaign, the employer announced it would be joining the national employer organization for the food sector – and the workers at Autogrill would benefit by being brought under the national agreement as a result.

* *LabourStart* was also asked to host an international online campaign in support of Georg Fischer workers in Turkey. The company was punishing members of the Lastik-Is union for trying to form a union. It was not our largest campaign, generating around 9,000 messages of protest and solidarity. But it was enough. The company was compelled to return to the bargaining table and sign a collective agreement with the union.

* A *LabourStart* campaign run jointly with the International Trade Union Confederation helped force the military dictatorship in Fiji to drop criminal charges against the country's trade union leaders.

Sometimes the campaigns we run trigger very hostile responses from companies.

A recent campaign against mining giant Rio Tinto triggered a very aggressive "cease and desist" letter from the company's U.S.-based lawyers.

The Autogrill campaign mentioned above also woke up the corporate lawyers, who threatened to take the union to court.

And even a small British-based charity had its lawyers threaten our web hosting company when we supported a campaign by a public sector union that was organizing workers at care homes it ran. When our web host panicked, we moved the campaign within 24 hours to an Australian site, using the domain name "wewillnotbesilenced.org".

Sometimes the companies decide to be clever and instead of caving in to our demands, or threatening us with legal action, they craft detailed responses to what we say in the campaigns and send these out to all our supporters. Unions need to be prepared for this sort of thing happening more and more in the future, as this is probably the smartest thing a company can do.

A few of our campaigns specifically target migrant workers. We've campaigned in support of "illegal" Burmese migrant workers in Thailand, and later in support of those same workers when they were being denied workers' compensation by the Thai government. We ran a campaign in support of South Korea's Migrant Workers Union. A recent campaign in the UK supported migrant workers working as cleaners in London. And we remain open to doing more such campaigns in the future.

While migrants haven't (yet) been the subject of many *LabourStart* campaigns, they have been the subject of many of the thousands of news stories posted every day to the website.

* * *

In addition to the online campaigns and the news service, *LabourStart* activists like to meet from time to time in the real world.

A first, small meeting took place in London in 2002, and this was eventually followed by ever-larger meet-ups that are now called "global solidarity conferences". These have been held in recent years in Washington, Hamilton (Ontario), Istanbul, Sydney and Berlin. The 2016 conference took place in Toronto.

The 2014 Berlin conference, in which nearly 400 trade unionists from all over the world participated, included a workshop on "Union Strategies towards migrants" organized by AK Undokumentierte Arbeit (Working group on undocumented workers) and several workshops on domestic workers, many of whom are also migrant workers.

* * *

More a loose network than a formal union structure, *LabourStart's* light-weight, flexible approach has allowed it to flourish and grow -- and help win victories for workers in many countries.

Father Peter Nguyen Cuong, a Maryknoll priest and executive director of the Vietnamese Migrant Workers & Brides Office in Bade City, Taiwan. *Photo credit: Joseph B. Atkins.*

CHAPTER FOUR

Moroccan Migrant Workers in Gibraltar Win Rights with Help from Friends

By

Daniel Blackburn

Director, International Centre for Trade Union Rights (ICTUR)

London, England

The Moroccans in Gibraltar arrived as a migrant workforce answering an urgent call for assistance by the Gibraltarian and British Governments at a crucial and testing time in the territory's history. Over the years, as the urgency of the labour supply problem faded, their historic contribution was poorly recognised and went unrewarded as the authorities allowed the Moroccans' immigration status to bar them from many of the rights and privileges enjoyed by their fellow Gibraltarians. Over the years the powerful local trade union Unite (formerly the TGWU) often worked with the Moroccans to challenge their second-class status. While a number of these struggles were successful, and some of the most notoriously discriminatory provisions were whittled away, the core problems remained as the authorities refused to take further reaching or more radical measures. But Unite did not abandon its struggle. In 2008, when Unite linked with the International Centre for Trade Union Rights (ICTUR), a new campaign was set in motion that rapidly accumulated an unstoppable momentum.

In February 2009 a delegation from ICTUR travelled to Gibraltar. The District Office of Unite provided every facility to support ICTUR's visit and organised an itinerary of meetings with the Moroccan Workers' Association, the Moroccan Community Association, Unite officials and representatives of the GGCA trade union, as well as arranging a series of invaluable meetings with political leaders. Unite also organised a public meeting to which members of the Moroccan community were invited to express their views. The participation in this meeting of hundreds of members of the Moroccan community demonstrated an immense level of dissatisfaction felt by the community about the situation. Following these events ICTUR worked with Unite and the Moroccan associations in what became an incredibly successful campaign. As we launched overlapping political, media and legal strategies designed to take best advantage of the linkages between the UK and Gibraltar the campaign began to draw in interest from the wider world, ramping up the pressure on the Gibraltar authorities to take action.

Within just a few years the situation of the Moroccans in Gibraltar was radically transformed, such that today most of the Moroccans in the territory enjoy the same rights as do their fellow Gibraltarians. In this chapter we explore how the Moroccans came to be in Gibraltar, we look at the problems they faced over the years, and we look at how the campaign to win their rights was implemented and the recent changes that have effectively ended their decades long situation as second-class citizens. The story is fascinating as it is a complete circle (from the first arrival of the Moroccans to their ultimate acceptance) and because it played out on the tiny scale of Gibraltar, which means that the steps and twists of the campaign, and factors of cause and effect, were relatively much easier to follow than would have been the case in a much larger territory with a wider range of actors.

Background: what brought the Moroccans to Gibraltar?

Gibraltar is a self-governing British overseas territory. With a population of roughly 30,000, it is a tiny peninsula of 6.5 square kilometres, including recently 'reclaimed' land at the southern tip of Spain. It overlooks the seaway dividing Europe and Africa. Throughout its history Gibraltar has been of major strategic military importance. The British Ministry of Defence used to employ more than 20 percent of the labour force. During the height of the cold war period funding from the United Kingdom Ministry of Defence represented 60 percent of Gibraltar's GDP.

For many decades Gibraltar was largely dependent upon the services of a large number of migrant workers in order to support industries associated with the military dockyards. Prior to 1969 the majority of these migrant workers were Spanish citizens, who crossed into Gibraltar on a daily basis from Southern Spain. In 1969 the Spanish authorities closed the border leaving a strategic military facility facing a severe crisis with shortages of several thousand workers who could not be replaced locally.

In response to the crisis, the Gibraltar and British Governments turned to the Kingdom of Morocco, just a few miles across the Straits. Thousands of Moroccan workers were recruited and encouraged to travel to Gibraltar and to take up employment with the Public Services Agency which managed construction, property and service operations around the naval dockyard. A ferry service was instigated direct from the Gibraltar waterfront, bypassing Spain to provide a regular and reliable service between Gibraltar and Morocco. Within nine months of the 1969 border closure the Moroccan migrant workforce consisted of at least three thousand workers.

The Moroccan experience in Gibraltar

For almost 40 years – and in some cases longer that this – Moroccan migrant workers have played an essential role in supporting the economy of Gibraltar by maintaining the dockyards. Despite paying taxes throughout this period, the great majority of the migrant workers were kept - by various measures – at arms length from many of the entitlements enjoyed by Gibraltarians. The Moroccans experienced problems with separation from their families, difficulties with travel on the local ferry, political disenfranchisement, barriers of access to housing, problems accessing non-emergency medical care, discrimination in the labour market, and difficulties and delays in accessing naturalisation processes. The Moroccans complained that they were barred from the subsidised public housing used by Gibraltarians, and, being unable to cross the border into Spain, they had only the options of crowding together in expensive private sector rental accommodation (if they could afford it, which many could not) or else falling into what passed for a poor social housing safety net, the badly-maintained, dirty, infested, unsafe and overcrowded 'hostels' that the ICTUR inquiry branded 'the Disgrace on the Rock'.

In spite of their immense contribution to the economic, social and cultural life of Gibraltar over a period of almost 40 years it is the unfortunate reality that the vast majority of Moroccan migrant workers faced shocking discrimination and violations of fundamental human rights. Whatever the reasons for this state of affairs and for the poor treatment of Moroccan workers in Gibraltar it was absolutely clear that the Government could not claim a poor economy as an excuse: the economy has diversified in recent years, branching out into financial services in particular, and for years Gibraltar has been booming.

It is important to emphasise, that the discrimination against Moroccan workers that we encountered is not a problem in the private sector, in employment, in the street, or in social interactions; rather it is a problem stemming directly from the public authorities. The problems we identified may be conveniently grouped together under five headings:

(i) Family re-unification: profound difficulties with visas and travel arrangements leading to prolonged separation of families.

(ii) Housing: discriminatory provision of public housing and poor quality of rented accommodation; and

(iii) Public services: ineligibility for certain welfare benefits, and discrimination in relation to health care;.

(iv) Political Rights: denial of the right to vote to people who have been living, working, and paying taxes in Gibraltar for up to 40 years;

(v) Naturalisation: allegations about slow, arbitrary, and discriminatory processing of applications for citizenship;

Family re-unification

One of the most direct and personal problems faced by the Moroccans, and a major complaint of the people we spoke with during our fact-finding visit, was that of separation from their families. We were told that the families of Moroccan migrant workers were only allowed to visit them in Gibraltar during the summer, and then only under tightly controlled circumstances. Children over 18 years of age were not allowed to visit at all, we were told, and when a spouse visited it was common practice that the visitor's passport would be confiscated for the duration of the visit. Those living in Gibraltar complained that the problem of separation from their families had been exacerbated over recent decades as what had once been a regular and reliable ferry service from Gibraltar to Morocco, which the Moroccans had used regularly, was cut back repeatedly, leaving only the barest minimum of a service.

The Deputy Chief Minister of Gibraltar agreed that the ferry service had been run down, that it was 'unreliable', that it ran only once per week, and that the 4 o'clock schedule could be delayed until midnight. Speaking with ICTUR he accepted that this was 'unsatisfactory'. Moroccans at a public meeting told us that the ferry was 'too expensive' and 'unpredictable', and complained that it was regularly cancelled'. They complained of having to 'wait for hours on the floor of the jetty in the baking sun with no proper facilities'. They said the conditions were 'degrading' and called for a waiting room to be provided. As non-EU citizens the Moroccans were unable to cross the border into Spain from where a nearby ferry port somewhat offered regular fast and reliable ferries connecting with Morocco.

We also heard individual cases of real hardship caused by this situation, including specifically the cases of the men who worked at the weekends, who had originally been able to visit their families regularly but who were now cut off for long periods, effectively unable to leave Gibraltar. Others found themselves unable to return to Morocco for urgent family reasons (such as a bereavement), although it was mentioned that the Spanish authorities had shown a willingness to allow Moroccans through the border in emergency situations. But it was not clear to us why relatively simple sensible arrangements could not be made in all cases to enable Moroccan workers to move freely between Gibraltar and Morocco, at their own convenience, as is the practice for other people.

Housing

The Moroccans also complained of discriminatory provision of access to accommodation. They claimed that they were being denied access to affordable public housing, and pointed out that such housing was available to Gibraltarians [1] at subsidised rates considerably below the private sector rental market. Given the scarcity and premium value of land in Gibraltar, combined with the impact of the booming economy, with this social safety net unavailable to them, the Moroccans faced a severe housing problem. Unable to afford the soaring rents for the attractive newly built private sector flats occupied by Gibraltar's high flyers, the Moroccans crowded together to rent small spaces within carved up and dilapidated old private sector housing. A community leader recently explained 'we had to get as many people in each place as possible to share that cost' [2]. A report issued by Sussex University in 2004 reported that almost all of the Moroccans lived ' in the oldest part of town, west of Main Street, the area of lowest quality housing. This iniquitous situation is maintained by the system of housing allocation, which bars access to government-owned housing to non-Gibraltarians' [3].

When I visited Gibraltar for a second time in early July, I was taken to see several examples of this accommodation, in each case apparently just a single small room, in some cases joining directly on to communal areas. I observed loose and rotten floorboards, poor ventilation and access to daylight, and bundles of electrical cable hanging loose from ceilings in private and communal areas. These 'rooms' in several cases had no door and were simply curtained off from public areas. A women of retirement age living in one such room (below ground level) described how this was the only housing available to her. A light well a few feet from the front of her room allowed a tiny stream of natural light into the cramped and dismal public area. She had worked for many years in Gibraltar, she told me, and had paid taxes to support the local economy. She complained of a lack of pension entitlements and told us that she continued to support herself by working in a restaurant. Her husband was dead, she told us, and she missed her family in Morocco. She explained that she would like nothing more than to return to Morocco, but she believed that she could not do so for financial reasons.

But the other option, far worse, was the shambolic, dirty and overcrowded semblance of a housing social safety net that existed in the form of the government-run Buena Vista hostel.

When our delegation visited the Buena Vista hostel one of the primary complaints raised by residents was that the rents paid, at £10 per week for two square metres of floor space, were considerably more expensive per square foot than government housing. There were 50 people living in cramped conditions. The hostel was dirty, paint was peeling from the walls, there were dozens of cockroaches and cobwebs. The tiny cubicles that represented the private space for each of the men were crammed together and represented a fire hazard: bare, untreated wooden walls and sheets of fabric were hung as rough 'doors'. In the public areas we observed fire extinguishers, but several of them difficult to access behind tables. Several residents complained of poor access to medical facilities for older residents and pointed out the obvious health risks, particularly for older residents, facing people living in such close, crowded and dirty conditions.

In 2007 British human rights campaigner Peter Tatchell visited the Buena Vista. He reported: 'It is decaying, cramped, dirty, infested, badly maintained and with poor amenities'. Tatchell continued: 'the rooms are tiny and cramped; half the showers and toilets are broken and unusable; sections of tiling have fallen off the walls in the bathrooms; the bare rough concrete floors in the toilets and showers are unhygienic; damp and mould affect many of the walls and ceilings; half the rings on the kitchen cookers do not work; only one sink per 13 residents; no heating in winter; laundry facilities are non-existent; much of the premises are infested with cockroaches; the hostel is poorly facilitated and supervised'. The ICTUR team observed an apparently identical catalogue of deprivation in its March 2009 visit to Buena Vista. We were unable to report any obvious changes or improvements since Peter Tatchell's visit in October 2007. The Deputy Chief Minister told us that, as a small community, Gibraltar faced restrictions of resources, though in our view this was difficult to square with the performance of the booming economy. Several politicians admitted that they were aware that the conditions at the Buena Vista were very poor indeed.

Public services

The Moroccan Workers Association told us that Moroccan workers had five yearly renewable residency permits if they were in work. If they lost their jobs they were entitled to remain under a six-month residency permit. Social security benefits were tied to citizenship status. Many welfare benefits were provided through a private social security company called Community Care, and, while the whole process and its rules were completely opaque to our team, it appeared to be the case that only Gibraltarians (i.e. – those with citizenship) were entitled to claim these benefits. The Moroccan Community Association complained that their members were workers and taxpayers, paying the same rates as Gibraltarian workers, and yet were not able to claim the same welfare entitlements as Gibraltarians.

Over the summer of our Inquiry, Unite the Union in Gibraltar arranged for a large group of Moroccans aged between 60 and 65 to apply for Community Care benefits. The applicants were only able to obtain application forms on the premises of Community Care and had to fill them out and hand them over immediately (despite Unite's best efforts ICTUR was unable to see an application form). The union informed us that the applications were all refused orally and that no written reasons were provided. We were assured by the Moroccan organisations that 'supplementary' or 'discretionary' benefits were known to exist, but we found it very difficult to find concrete information about them, as we were unable to find any reference to them on any publicly available social security forms. Eventually we found an official report acknowledging the existence of such benefits: the British Government's Fifth Periodic Report to the UN ICESCR Committee made passing reference to 'discretionary' social assistance measures in Gibraltar that were 'not supported by specific legislation'.

The Moroccan Workers Association also claimed that when their families visited during the summer they were unable to use health services, despite the fact that they were family members of lawfully resident long-term workers and taxpayers. As *The Guardian* newspaper reported: 'Moroccans also have reduced health cover. While Gibraltarians fly to Britain for serious illnesses that cannot be treated in Gibraltar, members of the Moroccan community have no such rights. Their taxes, they complain, pay for services reserved for others'. [4] Access to Spain for medical attention was raised as an additional difficulty. The Association said that a hospital card allowed migrants access to Cadiz hospital in Spain in 'very serious' cases but complained that in less serious cases Moroccans faced at least a '10 day wait for permission' to enter Spain for medical attention. In an almost unbelievable bureaucratic shambles it was necessary for Moroccan patients who were not very seriously ill to fly to the UK from Gibraltar airport in order to visit the Spanish Embassy in London so as to obtain a Spanish visa. EU law, we were told, now requires Moroccans to be in possession of a Visa to enter the Schengen territory (even to nip over to Algeciras – just a few minutes from the border – to catch a Morocco-bound ferry). Spain, we were informed, only issued such visas in London, and required the physical presence of the applicant, thus making it impractical and costly. [5]

In addition to questions relating to health care and pensions and welfare entitlement, we also heard complaints about access to education. Among several case studies provided to our delegation were details of a man whose two school-age children were undocumented, though resident in Gibraltar, living with their father (and apparently also with their mother, though her status was not clear from the information we were given). The children, we were told, were unable to access schools because of their undocumented status. The father had been corresponding with the authorities, and he admitted that his children did not have Gibraltarian ID cards, but had called for them to be allowed to access schooling. He had offered to pay fees. This issue was raised by the *Guardian* investigation:

'For a long time Said Ben Addel Hanin, a caterer, brought his wife and children to stay every other month. Over a year ago he kept them in Gibraltar. 'I work weekends, so I can't go to Morocco more than a few times a year. My wife does not want to be alone with the children. All we ask is for them to be with their parents. The government, however, wants them to leave. It has failed to school his eldest son, seven-year-old Oualid, even though he is of compulsory school age'. [6]

Political rights

An absolutely scandalous situation also persisted in the denial of the right of the Moroccans to participate in the civil and political life of their adopted home. For these workers, many of whom have been lawfully resident in Gibraltar for their entire working lives, the denial of democratic participation was the most striking manifestation of the discrimination against their community. These long-term residents have paid taxes and contributed to society over extraordinary periods of time. Many migrant workers attempted to register but had their applications turned down on the basis of nationality. Both the MWA and the MCA presented ICTUR with copies of written claims for registration on the electoral roll that had been presented by workers and tax-payers who had been resident in Gibraltar for periods of 31 years, 35 years, 36 years, and 40 years respectively. The Electoral Office Registration Officer replied simply and formally in each case: 'I intend to disallow your application...on the following grounds...you are a Moroccan national'.

As the Moroccans discussed the political situation with the ICTUR delegation and with Gibraltar's politicians, Unite formed a plan of action and decided to drag the denial of political participation out into the public realm and make it clear for all to see. And so on June 4, the day of pan-European elections, the Moroccan community and the local section of Unite picketed every polling station in Gibraltar. Unite union banners and placards were held aloft demanding the right for all to have a say in the election of the territory's representatives. And alongside the formal balloting process an informal election was also taking place, organised by the community. Unite's Gibraltar office was transformed into a mock polling station where ballots cast by the disenfranchised Moroccan community were counted in a process overseen by UK constitutional expert and public law professor Keith Ewing. At the close of polling, with mock ballots cast by some 70 percent of the Moroccan nationals resident in Gibraltar, the ballot box was marched through the streets and delivered to the Government offices, its passage into the counting hall blocked, as expected, by the police.

Of course, there had been no expectation that the mock ballots would ever be included in the official count, but a critical point was made in a very public demonstration: the depth of the community's desire to exercise the vote was undeniable. The mock papers were verified and counted the following day under the supervision of the Mayor of Gibraltar, although the results themselves were hardly relevant: this was a vote for change. In a year in which the world looked to America and the election of President Barack Obama as a stunning vindication of the goals of the 1960s civil rights movement, the hard-working taxpayers of the Gibraltar Moroccan community recalled the early slogan of colonial-era America 'taxation without representation is tyranny'.

Naturalisation

As rapidly became apparent to our delegation, the simple key to all of the problems encountered by the Moroccans was naturalisation: if the Moroccans were granted citizenship of Gibraltar they would enjoy rights and privileges on equal terms with the wider population. But unfortunately, the naturalisation process was itself the focus of yet another complaint, widely echoed by those we spoke with. It was related to us that Moroccans resident in Gibraltar for long periods of time (including in some cases 40 years or more) had struggled to obtain naturalisation. While a small number of applications were granted each year, the people we spoke to complained of slow, arbitrary and discriminatory application processes for citizenship. Most of those we spoke to were aware of these allegations, and it was widely admitted (even, privately, by political representatives) that unofficial policies were applied to applications, with political representatives from all parties hinting that they believed 'unofficial quotas' might be in use. The application process, we were told, is 'slow and mysterious'. Older, retired workers, we were told, were now leaving, returning home to Morocco, and no new workers were arriving. Some were of the opinion that naturalisation could be a fast process, particularly, they suggested, for men without children. The process might be achieved for those applicants within two years of making an application. But these cases were the exception. It was also suggested to us that not all persons classed as 'non-EU citizens' had problems obtaining Gibraltarian citizenship. One politician told us that people who he referred to as 'tax-exiles' from Russia, Canada and America 'have no problem getting status and a passport'.

The campaign for change

When the ICTUR delegation made its initial visit to Gibraltar, the local press showed considerable interest, with the Gibraltar Chronicle covering both the visit of the ICTUR delegation and the public meeting called by Unite and the migrant workers' associations. Articles appeared on 14th and 21st of February. On our return to the UK the ICTUR team wrote to *The Guardian* newspaper. Our letter was published on the 12th of March [7]. We relayed this information to contacts in Gibraltar and the fact that *The Guardian* was now covering the story was the also reported locally in the *Gibraltar Chronicle* as a story in itself. In fact, more was to come, as a journalist working with *The Guardian*, Giles Tremlett, was intrigued and decided to conduct his own investigation, published as the cover story to one of the supplement sections in a Saturday edition of the paper [8]. Tremlett's article largely coincided with our concerns [9]. As the feedback loop between the UK and Gibraltar press cycled the issue up the political agenda Gibraltar news organisation *Vox* announced that these developments threw 'an international spotlight' on the plight of what it termed Gibraltar's 'second class citizens'. [10] Adding to the spiralling media escalation, a young Polish journalist working on migration within the EU saw the report featured in *The Guardian* and contacted ICTUR. I subsequently met him in Gibraltar as he filmed a documentary about the situation, to be syndicated to public television companies throughout Europe. We never heard directly how the government had taken the presence of a Polish film crew in Casemates Square, but international film crews arriving in small communities and asking difficult political questions do not go unnoticed.

The constitutional situation of Gibraltar threw up other opportunities to frame the problem internationally, and it was possible for us to place some pressure on the Gibraltarian authorities by working with the British Parliament. We secured a meeting with the Chair of the All-Party Gibraltar Group in the British Parliament, and we also presented submissions to an inquiry that happened to be underway into the human rights obligations of British overseas territories under the House of Commons Foreign Affairs Committee. [11] In these interactions ICTUR called on the British government to take urgent steps to bring about an improvement in the human rights conditions of the Moroccans, arguing in particular that a moral debt was owed, dating back to the role that the Moroccans had played in providing vital assistance to an important British military facility in the 1960s and 70s, in addition to noting the apparent discrepancies between the UK's human rights commitments under international law and the situation in Gibraltar.

With the issue thus alive in both national and international parliamentary and media forums, ICTUR turned its attention to its primary area of expertise: the law. In order to ensure that the legal potential was investigated to its fullest potential ICTUR commissioned formal legal advice from one of the UK's leading discrimination barristers, Karon Monaghan, QC. Crucially, as we were aware, Ms Monaghan already possessed rights of audience in Gibraltar, and her expertise on discrimination law was well known there. Ms. Monaghan's Advice confirmed the views of ICTUR's in-house legal team, drew our attention to further aspects of discrimination law, and outlined a series of specific possible practical steps open to the campaigners in seeking to challenge what was clearly a discriminatory situation.

In meetings with political leaders, ICTUR addressed the question of extending rights of the Moroccan community in Gibraltar, and raised specifically the question of the ferry. The leaders acknowledged that the ferry service was 'unreliable' and 'unsatisfactory'. Representatives of the Government indicated that steps had been taken in meetings with the ferry company with a view to improve the service, while accepting the difficulties faced by the ferry operators. It was believed by several of those we spoke to that the best way forward would be for the Spanish authorities to make some sort of access available for Moroccans to allow them to make use of the Spanish ferry services. We agreed.

The inaccessibility of information permeated each area we investigated. As well as key guidance on housing and social security being classed as 'not public documents', we encountered suggestions of similar practices taking place within immigration, where it was alleged: i) that informal and unpublished criteria have been applied to naturalisation applications; ii) that the application process, decision-making procedures and timescales for responding to applications are opaque; and iii) that the 'custom' of only permitting family visits for Moroccans for a short period in the summer is not founded in law and therefore constitutes an application of informal criteria to the decision-making process.

The problems encountered by the Moroccans were compounded by an extraordinary lack of transparency and secrecy about matters that ought to be easily accessible. When I visited Gibraltar in July I attempted to obtain more information about the so-called 'supplementary benefits' and 'discretionary benefits' about which the Moroccan community had complained. It was only with considerable effort that I obtained a copy of the Ministry of Family, Youth, and Community Affairs, Department of Social Security Guide to Social Insurance (dated 2007). Even then the details remained obscure. We found no evidence of any formal application process, nor of the criteria to be applied to the assessment of such case.

Following our return to the UK, and in the wake of considerable media attention, we were informed of a new commitment to facilitate access to Spanish ferry ports by the Moroccan community. A tripartite ministerial 'forum of dialogue' held in Gibraltar on July 21, 2009, brought together Chief Minister Peter Caruana, Spanish Foreign Minister Miguel Angel Moratinos, and British Foreign Secretary David Miliband. The Forum communiqué set out a commitment 'to facilitate, by legally feasible practical solutions, the granting of Visas to the Moroccan community members resident in Gibraltar for transit through Spain towards their country'. As well as recognising the visa-related problems the communiqué sets out as one of its key aims an intention to bring about a negotiated solution to the problem imposed by EU visa rules that have proven such an arbitrary and unfair restriction on the right of the Moroccans to visit their loved ones just a few miles away. The communiqué confirms that the three Governments are motivated in this matter by 'humanitarian motives' and a commitment to 'good neighbourliness'.

A situation transformed

The real breakthrough came with the election of a new government in Gibraltar. Under an energetic new young leader, Fabian Picardo, the Gibraltar Socialist Labour Party moved decisively upon assuming office in April 2011. Within a year reforms had made it easier for more than 200 non-resident Moroccan nationals to collect their pensions, by introducing a visa waiver policy for this group. In 2013 the government amended the Immigration, Asylum and Refugee Act to wave visa requirements for nationals of specified countries. Moroccans who hold valid Schengen visas [12] were the first group specified, and they were permitted to enter for up to 21 days without further permission. This dramatically improved the possibility for Moroccan families to visit their loved ones in Gibraltar. Explaining the changes Chief Minister Fabian Picardo said 'Gibraltar has had a long and rich relationship with the Kingdom of Morocco and its people. For many years, however, we have failed to progress the relationship from the provision of labour by Moroccan nationals'. Picardo added that the new visa initiative would not only address historic barriers but would also open up the prospects for cross-border trade with Morocco. And also under Picardo steps were taken to sweep away the old lack of transparency and system of 'unofficial quotas' surrounding citizenship applications. In October 2013 ICTUR requested statistics on the naturalisation of Moroccans from the Gibraltar Government. The response was thrilling: 554 out of 596 'registered' Moroccans, we were told, had been naturalised 'so far', and the process was ongoing.

Chief Minister Picardo and his GSLP government have adopted the correct approach to dealing with all of the problems raised in ICTUR's report. It has tackled head on the problems of transparency and discrimination in the processing of naturalisation requests. This was a simple and effective approach, and it has reaped real rewards for the Moroccans, many of whom now find that all of the problems have ebbed away: as natural citizens of Gibraltar they can cross the borders freely, use the airport, access the ferries, and have full rights to a wide range of social entitlements and political freedoms, such as social security, medical attention, and the right to vote in elections. All parties indicated that the naturalisation process was still ongoing, and that more naturalisations were expected. In a further much needed action the new Government acquired premises, a former motel, which it planned to re-develop into more appropriate permanent home for the residents of the Buena Vista hostel. The new development, the government promises, 'will put an end to the inadequate living conditions that these residents of Buena Vista have had to endure for many years'.

In September 2013 Daniel Blackburn and Professor Keith Ewing travelled to Gibraltar to participate in an unrelated conference (concerning labour law reform). While we there we were able to speak with Unite and with members of the local Moroccan community. Both the union and the Moroccans told us that rapid and far-reaching change had occurred in Gibraltar since the ICTUR report. Legacies of the long-standing discriminatory regime persist. While the situation for 'registered Moroccans' has improved immeasurably we have found less clarity about the situation for Moroccans living in Gibraltar who were unregistered, and we have no information about how many people may be within this category. And while many Moroccans are now able to join the public housing waiting list, the housing shortages in Gibraltar remain a real problem and for many year to come many Moroccans are likely to be stuck in the overcrowded and outdated private-rental housing sector. As recently as September 2015 a Moroccan man died in a fire in a building in the densely populated inner-part of town, from which it was reported that more than 20 people had to be evacuated.

But on the whole there is a tremendous optimism and an overwhelming certainty from the Moroccan representatives that we spoke with that things have changed at a fundamental level. Giving an interview to *Panorama* (a local newspaper), Mohammed Sasri, a Moroccan, was quoted as saying: 'Nowadays under the GSLP/Liberal administration things are a lot better for the 900 or so Moroccans that currently live in Gibraltar. We now feel we have a bit of dignity as around 80 percent of us have acquired British citizenship with some families being reunited with relatives in Belgium, France or Spain for the first time'. Sasri continued: 'Young people are much more integrated into the community, with Moroccans working for the general public as civil servants, lawyers or businesspeople. The children who at one time hid from the police so they would not be deported are now policemen ... , confirming that Gibraltar is a unique place in a world where our tolerance and co-existence is unlike any other place in the world.' [13] Confirming this new spirit of inclusivity, the 2015 Gibraltar World Music Festival was themed to 'celebrate cultures of Maghreb and Morocco'.

Diego Reyes Jr., organizer with Farm Labor Organizing Committee, and Diego Reyes Sr., a migrant farm worker in Sanford, North Carolina, USA. Both are natives of Mexico. *Photo credit: Joseph B. Atkins.*

THE MIDDLE EAST

CHAPTER FIVE

Two Years Turn into Twenty One: "Temporary Migrants" in Israel Answer Back through Local Activism

By

Angie Hsu

Activist for Migrant Workers, Tel Aviv, Israel

"Filipina! Filipina! Will you marry me?"
"Why do you want to marry me? You don't even know me."
"I am looking for a good wife to stay home, cook, take care of the house. You know, these Israeli women...they want to study and work. I need a good Filipina, Asian wife, like you."

In fact, I'm not Filipina. But apparently in Israel, I look "Filipina enough" to prompt these types of exchanges. From my first visit to Israel in 2007, these strange interactions began to make me wonder about the lives of the real Filipinas living in Israel, many of whom are employed as caregivers. As I met more of them, I asked for their advice: How do you respond to these comments? What is the best way to avoid these situations? How do you deal with the fact our faces ("exotic" and "Eastern") often take precedence over our personalities, our backgrounds, and more? When I eventually moved to Israel, the advice of "veteran" Filipinas who had lived in Israel for 10, 15 or even 20 years turned out to be more useful to me than that of fellow young Americans (most of whom are Jewish and moved to Israel for a variety of reasons). What was even more important was the opportunity to listen to the stories of these women, who fell somewhere on the spectrum between "temporary" migrant workers and long-term residents of Israel.

In many ways, their experiences reflect that of migrants around the world: the government often sponsors their entry but fears that they will stay; they play a significant role in the labor market but receive limited recognition; they participate in society but are rarely seen as members of society. But something else always piqued my curiosity. In Israel, a self-defined Jewish State that actively strives to prevent non-Jewish immigration, non-Jewish migrants who find themselves legally here for years and years, even decades, still face the threat of being stripped of status, and even deportation. Even after 20 years of residence, permanent status and citizenship remain impossible in most cases, and these women's stay in Israel is seen as "temporary" by the State authorities. Even in cases in which they do receive status, daily experiences such as the one described above are constant reminders of their migrant identity. As non-Jewish, non-native Israelis, how do these long-term residents participate in Israeli civil society?

The answer is, not surprisingly, different for each individual who finds herself in this position. In South Tel Aviv, where migrant worker and asylum seeker communities are most organized in Israel, there are various examples in which veteran migrant workers have turned to different forms of activism as a means of embracing their contradictory statuses of "outsider" (migrant worker) and "insider" (long-term resident). After a brief background to further contextualize the situation in Israel, this chapter follows four different efforts in which long-term Filipina migrants have found meaningful ways, through local activism, to negotiate their complex identities as insiders/outsiders and to assert their unique role in Israeli society.

Background

The State of Israel began recruiting migrant workers in the late 1980s and early '90s, due to a combination of factors, the first being the financial incentives of recruiting foreign labor. Not only were migrant workers willing to accept lower salaries than Israelis, but given the lack of governmental enforcement of labor law for migrant workers, employers could more easily exploit workers for their personal financial interests. The second, unique to Israel, was the claim that Palestinian workers previously employed within Israel now posed a security threat during and following the First Intifada (a Palestinian uprising against the Israeli occupation of the West Bank, East Jerusalem and Gaza). Today, migrant workers are employed in the sectors of caregiving, construction, agriculture, and restaurants; the first three sectors depend heavily on foreign labor. Over 100,000 migrant workers are employed in Israel with visas; the largest group of them are the 50,000 caregivers for the sick and elderly, 80 percent of whom are female. About half of caregivers in Israel are from the Philippines. The rest are from Nepal, India, Sri Lanka, Moldova, and a number of Eastern European countries.

Filipina women constitute the largest group of migrant workers in Israel, a visibility so impressionable that the word for Filipina in Hebrew, *Filipinit*, is now synonymous with the word *metepelet*, or "caregiver." The *Filipinit* does not represent Filipina women, but generally for female migrant caregivers from various developing Asian countries. Given the dependence of the Israeli State on migrant workers for caregiving, a great many Israeli families have had experience with migrant caregivers in some capacity. It is important to note that not all Filipinas in Israel are caregivers; many Filipinas also work as housecleaners in private homes, especially if they no longer hold a caregiving visa.

While Israel grants automatic citizenship to all Jewish immigrants according to the 1950 Law of Return, Israel does not have any laws or regulations that relate to long-term status for non-Jewish residents. So while migrant caregivers in Israel have the possibility to stay employed in Israel indefinitely (under very specific terms), they never receive any additional social rights whatsoever as a long-term resident. This is fueled by Israel's ongoing concerns about maintaining the Jewish demographic majority of the country, and hence avoiding naturalization of non-Jewish residents. It has resulted in what Professor Adriana Kemp of Tel Aviv University calls a "new social stratum of non-citizens, whose transience is anchored in law, even though some of them have become de facto 'permanent temporary residents.'" In addition to this group, there also exists in Israel a group of veteran Filipinas who were able to receive temporary or permanent residency status, the result of the struggle to protect the rights of children born to migrant workers.

The Rights of Our "Israeli Children"

"When did you get involved with activism?"
"Since the struggle, in 2006...to give my grandson status. Of course, I went with them to the demonstrations, to the rallies, I invited people to join...I say now, 'In my own country I wasn't an activist. When I come to another country, I become an activist." - *Angie Robles*

Angie Robles has lived in Tel Aviv for close to 25 years, even though she wasn't even sure she would complete her two-year contract when she first arrived at Ben Gurion Airport just outside of Tel Aviv. Her life has included various surprises, such as experiencing the First Intifada while employed in Ramallah and raising her grandson (who was born in Israel) after his father - her son - suddenly passed away. She described to me how she never questioned her own lack of citizenship in Israel, but when challenges arose facing her grandson's status, Robles became part of an activist community of migrant worker parents, predominantly Filipina mothers who had lived in Israel for many years.

The struggle that Robles mentions was to fight deportation of children born to migrant workers in Israel and for granting of legal status to the children and their families. In 2006, 900 children and 2,300 of their family members received legal status (permanent residency for the child and temporary residency for parents and siblings). The child had to have been born in Israel or lived in Israel for at least six years; their parents must have entered Israel legally; and the child had to speak Hebrew "and thus their deportation would constitute cultural exile," in the words of Hotline for Migrants and Refugees. At age 21, if the child completed army service, he would then be able to apply for citizenship, and the parents and siblings would receive permanent residency. In 2009, the government announced it would begin detaining and deporting undocumented children and their families starting in August, right after the end of the school year. Up until this point, there had been an unspoken agreement against the deportation of Israeli-born children of migrant workers.

Maya Peleg, then a social worker at MESILA (Aid and Information Center for Migrant Workers and Refugees), and Rotem Ilan, a volunteer with MESILA, began organizing meetings to discuss the impending deportations. At their first planning meeting, they expected some 20 migrant parents to show up, and were shocked when in flooded over 150. Committees were organized, including ones focused on media outreach, gathering parliamentary support, organizing rallies and doing constant fieldwork (such as tracking immigration police presence and crackdowns in South Tel Aviv). The Israeli support was also significant, including that of recognized Israeli politicians and celebrities. Robles shared this: "Because people are fighting for your rights...also, I am fighting for [my] rights, you have to join. It's not nice that they are fighting for you and you are just sitting there." This cause, more than some others, showcased migrants and Israelis joining together. For activists like Robles, it gave a sense of belonging to a bigger community in Israel, one that accepted both Israeli "insiders" and Filipina "outsiders."

A strong force in the struggle was the Moms Committee, a Filipina women's leadership group. Not only did members of the Moms Committee already have trained leadership skills from MESILA, but it was clear that the Filipina communities were the most organized and ready to rally supporters. The Moms Committee had developed out of Coffee Plus, a group of Filipina women that had been meeting weekly for nearly three years, discussing intense and emotional subjects under the guidance of Peleg. One member of the Moms Committee and Coffee Plus said, "I didn't feel like I'm activist, but I feel like I'm just helping the children...they should have [status]...to live like a normal individual, not [with] the police, the immigration, coming after, knocking on the door." The beginnings of the Committee (and its members) were quite humble; the very name of the group pointed straight at their identities as moms whose activism was rooted in the very real and immediate need to help their own children.

Ilan, who mentored the Moms Committee, describes the energy and passion of these women, who were tireless in their commitment to the cause: "It was amazing, the number of people who came to these demonstrations was unbelievable...Think about their lives, a mother who works now for 12 hours a day in housekeeping, works all day long, takes care as a single mother of her child because the dad was deported, and yet has time to go and arrange with us a demonstration and go fight for her right."

The struggle directly led to the founding of the non-profit Israeli Children under Ilan's leadership, an organization that fights against deportations and advocates for legal status for the children and their families. The name was chosen to emphasize how these children were born in Israel, speak Hebrew, and could face serious trauma in being forcibly removed from Israel, the only home they knew. In this way, this struggle gave legitimacy to the activists' complex identities as migrant/resident, insider/outsider. The argument was that their children were Israelis, and hence their mothers had a legitimate role and reason to be in Israel as well. In Israel, migrant workers and their children have repeatedly been labeled as a demographic threat to the Jewish State. Eli Yishai, who was the minister of the interior from 2009 to 2013, publicly stated that female migrant workers "have to be deported before they become pregnant" to prevent their "taking root" in Israel (a term used by the Ministry of Interior). Similarly, the policies of the Ministry of Interior ban migrant workers from being in an intimate relationship with each other. If their relationship is uncovered, one or both of them will be deported.

In 2010, Israeli Children and all of the community groups involved celebrated when the government again made a "one-time humanitarian gesture" in which about half of the families who applied for status succeeded. Today, given the current political climate, it was decided by Israeli Children that protests and rallies were no longer the most strategic use of time and resources, so the organization currently focuses on the pending cases, filing appeals and overseeing ongoing applications. Some of the original Moms Committee members are still involved in the work of Israeli Children. For example, even though Miranda (who asked that her real name not be used) already has status for herself and her son, she said, "The feeling that you got your [status] but some of them don't have...You want to fight for somebody else, so at least they can experience what you experience, the freedom."

As Robles said, these activities become a gateway for migrant workers to learn more about rights, not just their children or grandchildren's, but their own as well. Right now, many of the children who received status are beginning to enter, and exit, the army and become recognized by the Israeli public as citizens. Very soon, we will see how the activism carried out in the past will affect their futures in Israel, as well as how Israel views itself and its demographics.

Creating a University for Themselves

As a resident of South Tel Aviv, I often have to defend our decision to live here. The general Israeli public sees these neighborhoods as crime and poverty-ridden due to the influx of migrants and refugees, even though - historically - the government neglected these areas and its predominantly Mizrahi Jewish population (Jews who are of Middle Eastern descent). I often explain that not only do I feel safe where I live, but it is one of the only parts of the city that feels truly international, where I am less often questioned with "Where are you from in the East?" or "My mother is sick...do you need a job?" Israelis are often surprised to hear these anecdotes; they are usually equally unaware of the various vibrant community projects that migrants are involved with in South Tel Aviv, in part because the governmental support and resources are more limited in this part of the city.

My apartment has a direct view of the Central Bus Station of Tel Aviv, a massive, nearly empty shell of a transportation hub. While the buses still run from there, many of the stores inside are empty and the whole place has the feel of a ghost town. However, it is deep inside the Central Station that you can find various resources for the migrant and refugee community, like the Health Clinic established specifically for migrant and asylum seekers and the office of the community organization, the African Refugee Development Center (ARDC). The Central Station also houses the CEC, as it's commonly known, or the Community Education Center. The CEC offers classes for migrant workers and refugees, designed to provide them with "knowledge and skills that will help them face the challenges of gaining status and living in Israel as well as the challenges of returning to their countries of origin if they choose (or are forced) to do so." The classes range from Hebrew and English to computer skills, fashion design to child psychology.

The CEC started from the Migrant Workers' Leadership Group of MESILA, an initiative that aimed to empower leaders from the different communities - including natives of the Philippines, Burma, South Africa, and even Mongolia - in preparation for the upcoming deportations of migrant mothers and their children. The course focused on ways to provide psychological support to the communities and also how they can represent themselves in the Israeli media. Upon its finish, Yael Mayer, who was facilitating the course as a staff member at MESILA, suggested the students organize a graduation ceremony. The students ran with the idea, and they arrived in dresses and tuxedos with a full program for the duration of the ceremony. Mayer recalls that Professor Gideon Kunda, who had been involved with the course, noted how the students actually made a graduation ceremony for themselves similar to the ones of large, recognized universities; they were creating the feeling of a university for themselves. Mayer and Kunda later went to the group to describe what they had witnessed and present the idea of establishing a community education center to continue the learning. The group quickly agreed to develop a model that would be the first accessible means of further education for migrant and refugee communities.

In one of the first activities, Mayer remembers teaching the leaders how to develop, run and analyze a survey, in order to poll their peers on what types of classes they would want to take. Hence, even though the process was new to them, the migrant leaders involved were "actually part of building this project." From there, the migrant-led leadership team developed positions, made enrollment forms, printed student ID cards and more. Mayer described it as "amazing because they [migrants] were president, accountant and everything and also after graduations, staying and cleaning up and making sure everything is perfect and preparing the signs...being a part of every small detail." She emphatically added that three of the original leaders, all of whom are Filipina, "were the engine of all of this."

The first semester included four classes and 80 students, and in six years it has grown in its professionalism and capacity to provide leadership and learning opportunities. There have been over 200 students and 12 classes each semester. The value of the CEC is not only providing migrants with practical skills but also the opportunity to share and acquire knowledge. Mayer described that for many students "it's feeling significant because 'I'm a student, not just a cleaner, I'm learning, I'm developing, I'm doing something I'm proud of, I'm progressing...' This is something many, many people talked about, and many of the Filipinos talked about: 'I'm finally developing myself.' It's also a way to negotiate with Israeli society, feeling that you're really part of something."

Robles was also one of the founders of the CEC. When I asked Robles if her involvement in Israeli Children and the CEC changed how she felt about Israel, she said, "There was a change. Because when I became an activist struggling for [my] rights, it's asking, 'Why do others get it and why not me?' And we are all the same. So...what's the difference? What they have, what we don't have...when we are all the same." The CEC, for its leaders and students, is a means of acknowledging they are a different and unique group (since they are not always eligible for study in Israeli universities or cannot attend day classes due to their jobs), but simultaneously claiming their right to education. Like Robles said, this is the same right for all people, no matter if they are migrants, refugees, or native Israelis. The CEC is a way to negotiate with Israeli society, as Mayer described, to both be a part of its education system (even informally) while acknowledging their migrant identities.

Mayer is now a clinical psychologist and draws on her profession to explain the significance of the CEC's model and its professionalism: "In psychology we call it transitional objects. Most of them didn't have Israeli IDs and they felt that this way they are excluded from Israeli society. All these concrete business cards and diplomas are like transitional objects [in psychology], that help them make the transition between their culture to the Israeli culture and something that opens the culture, the Israeli side, before them and says, 'Look, you are part of it.' To be able to create something new in a place where they are strangers. And to create something new in that place, you are not such a stranger

anymore. You are part of it. You own it. You created it yourself."
One of the original leaders, who was eventually deported back to
the Philippines, recently shared on Facebook, "I'm proud to be one
of those who founded CEC & hoping that whoever (is) left will
continue the journey what we had started." Six years later, the CEC
is still going strong and providing a space for creation and
belonging for the migrant community.

Friday Night Dinner for All

One Saturday night, I was invited to attend a gathering held by
the local activist and pastor Miranda. Right before I entered the
building, I realized I was experiencing a truly unique moment in
Israel: I was standing next to the Kingdom of Pork store and
hearing a chorus of voices above me singing "Praise Jesus" to
amplified drums and keyboard. It was the weekly service of the
Love of Christ Parish in South Tel Aviv. Love of Christ Parish has
an extremely diverse congregation, which makes it stand out from
the plethora of other churches in South Tel Aviv; Nigerian, Indian,
Kenyan, and Filipino members hold services in English, though
one could hear several different languages as they prayed quietly to
themselves and greeted friends in their own language. It is one of
the rare examples of the migrant and refugee/asylum seeker
communities coming together and creating a new mixed, support
network.

In 2002, most of the migrant men without status were
deported, which led to a sudden disappearance of many of the male
pastors. There was then a shift to introduce women into positions
as pastors, such as Miranda. She came to Israel in 1995, also with
the intention of only staying two years. She is involved in the
church (as a pastor now), her son's school, various activist groups,
and also finds the time to run the Friday night outdoor "soup
kitchen" in Levinsky Park.

Levinsky Park, directly across the Central Bus Station, is
one of the central social hubs of the asylum seeker community.
Dotted around the park's perimeter are Eritrean coffee shops and
Indian and Asian grocers. In addition to reflecting the extreme
poverty of the asylum seeker community (sleeping bags next to the
slides and swings are rolled up during the day, and rolled out

during the night), Levinsky Park is a common choice for public events, such as the protests organized by Israeli Children mentioned above. Every Friday night, volunteers gather around giant vats and pots of food - donated by Israeli businesses before closing for the Sabbath - and drive it from Central Tel Aviv to the South. There, Love of Christ Parish members and other volunteers dish out the food for low-income and homeless residents of South Tel Aviv, asylum seeker and Israeli alike. The feedings are coordinated with the Israeli non-profit organization Leket, which is the country's National Food Bank and largest food rescue network. In this way, the migrant volunteers in Levinsky Park are also a part of a large, recognized Israeli organization. As we were looking at pictures together, one of them proudly pointed out how they had been given T-shirts with the Leket logo. Their involvement with this cause places them both at the center of the migrant and refugee community, and also with a greater Israeli effort to fight hunger nationwide. Volunteering in the Levinsky Park affirms and values their identities as both migrants and residents of Israel.

The mood is lively and filled with laughter, volunteers (the vast majority of them long-time residents of Israel) greeting each other and cracking jokes. It is a true show of camaraderie. While the migrant and asylum seeker communities face very different challenges (and each community includes several distinctly different sub-groups), the reality is they are often lumped together by the Israeli public. Asylum seekers are most commonly referred to as "foreign workers" or, even worse, economic "infiltrators." One of the Filipina volunteers said to me that the refugee volunteers are "nice, good people, friendly. Part of our situation is similar." Despite the fact that these individuals face endless challenges and discrimination, they find the time, energy and compassion to come together and volunteer their Friday nights.

Leila Manzano Ayat has lived in Israel for 21 years (the chapter's title references her unexpected life in Israel) and is extremely busy. Between her job and volunteering on Friday nights, she is also active in her university fraternity's Israeli branch in Tel Aviv. They visit sick Filipinos who are alone in the hospital, pick up trash along the beach, and they have traveled to Jerusalem to give free health screenings to other Filipino migrant workers. Why is she involved in local activism and community efforts? She said it makes her feel more like a part of Israeli society. "I want to do more, I want to show them [Israelis] we are worth it...that we are not a waste...we are also useful. That's why I keep volunteering." But Leila also emphasized that it simply "feels good": "You help people, you feel good. You don't need to please everybody or prove to everybody...as long as you enjoy. And I feel good doing it."

Using Facebook to Fight for Labor Rights

"We have a lot of ways of communication nowadays. We have the Internet, we have the social media, we have the cell phone, we have text messages...it's how you utilize what you have." - Cheryl Sevegan

When Israel was founded as a state, protective labor laws were enacted that were considered relatively progressive at the time. However, in reality, migrant caregivers face exploitation and abuse, and are among the most marginalized workers in Israel. The caregiving sector is extremely unique in Israel because it is the only sector in which migrant workers can technically stay in Israel under certain circumstances for an unlimited period of time. Hence, the population of migrant caregivers in Israel is extremely diverse in terms of their length of stay in Israel, and likewise in terms of their awareness about their labor rights. Kav LaOved (Worker's Hotline) is an Israeli non-profit organization dedicated to protecting the labor rights of disadvantaged groups, and is extremely well-known in the migrant caregiver community. Kav LaOved has become a platform for migrant workers to demand the upholding of their labor rights.

On June 23, 2014, Kav LaOved posted on the Facebook group "Kav LaOved - Migrant Caregivers" (which has nearly 30,000 followers) an update that read, "Today, a Supreme Court hearing will take place to discuss rights, including social security and health insurance, for caregivers who have been living and working in Israel for over 10 years. This is very exciting, as our original petition on this issue was filed back in 2006." The petition was made possible by the testimonies of several long-term caregivers who opened up to Kav LaOved about their experiences in Israel. The post was shared 540 times, and caregivers replied with enthusiastic messages like the following:

"It is a struggle, but we will do whatever we can to try and fight it. Of course, we will need your help and support...thanks a lot kav laoved...!!
this is one step forward for the campaign on equal rights. we must be united as migrant workers
we do hope and pray that all your innitiative [sic], efforts and struggles shall prevail in fighting and pursuing to alter any rules that supress [sic] and violate the basic rights of migrant workers here in Israel! let's join hand-in-hand! God Bless Us All!"

The Supreme Court petition was accepted in part, but actual implementation of the decision continues to develop. Judge Barak-Erez's statement in the verdict closely mirrored the stance of Kav LaOved and workers themselves: "These are people who stay in the country for many years, legally and under the state's request and blessing. Now, when these caregivers need to be taken care of, they must be treated generously and be allowed to heal and regain their strength."

Cheryl Sevegan has been a caregiver in Israel for over 11 years. In this time she has been able to host seminars on caregivers' rights, lecture at Israeli universities, write cover stories for local Filipino magazines, and represent Filipinas in Israel through serving on the Federation of Filipino Communities in Israel, the European Network and the Global Filipina Diaspora. Cheryl's employers are remarkably supportive of her activism, which allows her to stay extremely connected and networked, including attending international conferences in Italy and the United States. Given all her years here, she says, "If someone has problems and asks help from me, it's much easier to reach out and help her because I already have connections...I already know what to do."

Caregivers are required to live with their employers in Israel, which means they often de-facto work around the clock six or seven days a week. Thus participating in activism is not the easiest of activities to fit into their schedule, especially if their employers are ailing and cannot be left alone at home or are not supportive of their activism. However, almost all caregivers do have cell phones and Internet. The digital age has provided a new platform for activism, and caregivers in Israel are no different. Caregivers are able to express their opinions and thoughts, and also feel the sense of community as others share and listen. Cheryl told me, "I use it [the Kav LaOved Facebook page] sometimes when I want to know updates. If I have friends asking me and I'm not sure about my answers, I always look for Kav LaOved's updates." The Internet not only allows Cheryl to be in touch with her friends but also to stay updated herself as an activist and local leader.

On several occasions Kav LaOved has also posted surveys on the page, with hundreds of caregivers quickly responding and sharing their experiences. Some of these surveys have gone on to act as the basis for future legislation to strengthen caregivers' rights, such as the struggle for inclusion of migrant caregivers in the Israeli Work and Rest Hours Law. Caregivers do not receive overtime pay since they are unprotected by the law. In effect, caregivers are making just $1.50 per hour, which is 25 percent of the legal minimum wage in Israel. In 2013, the High Court of Justice rejected Kav LaOved's appeal to apply the law to caregivers. In response, the organization drafted new legislation with Parliament members and simultaneously organized a 10-week workshop about labor rights, in which new and veteran migrant workers took part. The language of Israeli labor law clearly applies to all workers, regardless of their nationality or status. This provides further support for migrant labor activists' claims that they are not fighting for "special treatment" as migrant workers, but rather to be treated the same as Israeli workers (such as receiving overtime pay). At the end of the workshop, and following extensive print and online media outreach targeting both the Israeli public and other caregivers, the participants organized a rally for equal rights attended by migrant workers and Israeli allies.

Marcia (who asked that her real name not be used) was one of the lead organizers of the rally in early 2014. Having been a teacher in the Philippines, she was a natural at meeting and connecting with each of her fellow activists at the beginning of each class, and finding common ground to unite the group as they planned the rally. In the end, she had to forgo attending the event she passionately worked on for over three months when her employer suddenly entered the hospital. Though the group had planned for her to be one of the main spokespeople to the press, other caregivers - like Cheryl - stepped up to the job and were able to still convey the stories and challenges facing caregivers in Israel.

Answering Back through Activism

"When I started joining this activist group with the human rights, I learned that everyone has their own rights. Wherever you are, you have your rights. Every human being has the right. You have the right to talk...the more you don't answer, the more they will put you down you all the time. So you need to answer them. You need to put yourself up." - Leila Manzano Ayat

One Sunday night, I was invited by Leila to join her and her friends for a coffee at the McDonald's in the Central Bus Station. It was only when I arrived that I learned that everyone there had been involved with the Moms Committee from over 10 years ago, and many of these women are involved with the different causes introduced above. The conversation jumped from topic to topic, a constant shift between Tagalog, Hebrew and English. Miranda said to me at one point, "The Moms Committee, we are still intact...you can see we are still complete." Over the course of several hours, they described to me how this group and others have taught them about human rights, leadership and activism, how they continue to be involved in the neighborhoods of South Tel Aviv that they have watched develop over 10 or even 20 years. They described how this group is their family in Israel, and their gatherings are not always for planning and organizing, but often to simply "talk and unwind." With this type of flexible and multi-faceted support, along with their years of experience, these Filipina women have developed the skills and confidence to face the complexities and challenges of Israel straight in the face, and to answer back through local activism.

* * *

I was often in awe at how casually these women spoke of their efforts (and achievements), as if it was as ordinary and day-to-day as brushing their teeth. But for many of them, these efforts were necessary for living their daily lives as migrants in Israel. Their activism was not driven by deeply-rooted ideology but rather their realities as they tried to work, find community, raise a family and educate themselves. In other words, these forms of activism are part of their process of living and belonging in Israel while still embracing their "outsider" status in some way. Their efforts contribute to their communities and Israeli society at large, and they are only made possible by the accumulated experiences and insights they hold as Filipina migrants residing long-term in Israel. To echo Leila's words, through local activism these women ensure that they are not being put down as foreigners or migrants; instead, they - as residents of Israel - are raising themselves and each other up.

ASIA

CHAPTER SIX

India's Movable Workforce

By

Sindhu Menon

"Don't look at me
As though I am an alien or a stranger,
Don't let the dagger of antipathy
Fly out of your eyes
I am your neighbor.
Don't call me a foe, an antagonist or a rival,
Don't roll up your mistrustful sleeves for a fight.
I am your friend.
Don't hold this murderous weapon in your kind hand,
Don't deny me the right to work, to eat, or to live.
I am your brother"

Demetrios Trifiatis (*We Are Brothers*)

On October 6, 2015, Kasthuri Munirathinam, a 58-year-old migrant labourer who hails from a remote village in Tamil Nadu, a southern state in India, lost her right arm. It was not an accident; her hands had been chopped off by an angry employer in Riyadh, Saudi Arabia, in the household where she worked as domestic maid. The so-called crime committed by Munirathinam was that she tried to escape from the workplace because she was unable to bear the ill-treatment and torture by her employers.

On December 16, 2013, Bialu Nial, 30, and Nilambar Dhangada Majhi, 35, from the Kalahandi district in Orissa, the eastern state in India, lost their right hands when a contractor and associate chopped them off after hours of confinement and torture. Both were migrant workers hired to work in the brick kilns of Chhattisgarh yet were forcefully taken to Andhra Pradesh. Here again, the crime was that they ran away, refusing to be transported to Andhra Pradesh instead of the promised Chhattisgarh.

On November 2, 2013, 34-year-old Rakhi Bhadra, hailing from North 24 Parganas District in the state of West Bengal, succumbed to torture from her employer. She had 28 injuries over her body, visible burn marks and injuries on the head, chest, stomach, arms and legs. She had been working as a domestic maid in Delhi for ten months. Her crime was that she demanded regular wages, decent food to eat, and drinking water.

The cases of Rakhi, Majhi, Nial and Munirathinam are not such a rarity in India, although it certainly is a rarity when such cases get attention. Migrant workers, the abysmal conditions in which a majority of them live and work, the exploitation and humiliations they undergo are all on rise, but unfortunately they remain a low priority to the government when it comes to addressing their issues.

Thus Speak the Statistics

In the Census of India, people are considered migrants when they are counted in a different place from their birthplace. The 2001 census report in India showed the total number of migrants at 314 million, of which 268 million were intra-state migrants, 41 million inter-state migrants, and 5.1 million migrants from outside the country.

The UNESCO report "Social Inclusion of Internal Migrants in India" estimates the current number of internal migrant workers in India to be around 400 million, approximately one third of India's population. Migrants who moved out of India to other countries are estimated at 11.4 million.

According to the National Sample Survey conducted by the Ministry of Statistics and Program Information, around 28 per cent of India's population migrate, and around 38 per cent of total migrants are in the labour market. Seventy per cent of them are males and 26 per cent females.

The Nature of Migration

The nature of labour migration can be assessed according to the degree and extent of vulnerability to which the migrant workers are exposed. Is the migration for survival, subsistence, sponsored, voluntary? On one hand, extreme economic and social hardships in rural areas can force workers to migrate for survival. On the other, seasonal unemployment and poverty may force many to migrate for subsistence, often for short periods, to nearby regions. The most dangerous vulnerability is the sponsored migration where the initiative emerges from an employer's preference for long-distance migrant workers. This often ends up with labourers hired through contractors/middlemen who get workers by paying advances that will later be deducted from their wages. Voluntary migration emanates from the migrant himself, who bears the cost of migration and expects to find employment with the help of relatives, friends, caste or village.

Poverty, landlessness, loss of livelihood, natural calamities, lack of opportunities, discrimination based on caste, marriage, etc., are major reasons for migration. Recently, with the increase in inter-state mobility, labour mobility has become more diverse with labour sending and receiving states on the increase and more and more sectors/avenues opening up for migrants. With 18.6 and 11.1 per cent respectively of their population living in villages, the North Indian states of Uttar Pradesh and Bihar have the highest population of migrants.

A large number of migrants are employed in sectors like agriculture, plantations, quarries, informal manufacturing, power looms, handlooms, construction, hotels, tourism, transport, garment manufacturing, fish processing, and food processing. Metropolitan cities like Delhi, Mumbai, and Kolkata are major destinations for interstate migrants. They are scattered all over as casual labourers, head-loaders, rickshaw pullers, cleaners, security guards, drivers, tailors, sex workers, brick kiln workers and domestic maids. They migrate, inter-state and intra-state, from rural to rural, rural to urban, urban to urban and urban to rural, of which rural to rural and rural to urban migration have been the predominant patterns of migration.

The Plight of Migrants

Seventy-year-old Ramu Kaka, as he is fondly known in his locale, is a ground nut hawker on the busy streets of Chandni Chowk, one of the oldest and busiest markets in Old Delhi. He migrated from Bihar 31 years ago when the 1984 flood devastated his village Hempur in the Saharsa district of Bihar. The flood affected half a million people and around 96 villages were engulfed. "I still remember that fateful day where all my crops, cattle, household properties got washed away by water along with my only son," recollects Ramu. "Along with my wife and three daughters, I tried re-building everything, but couldn't and so I had to migrate in search of a job. When a distant relative from Delhi visited our village and offered to take me along, I did not hesitate and from that day onwards I am living in Delhi. I worked as a construction labourer, rickshaw puller, hotel boy for survival." He lives in a one-room tenement in a slum in Old Delhi and for the last 10 years he has been selling ground nuts. He visits his family every six months and makes sure to be there for harvesting.

Extended working hours, poor wages, bad working and living conditions, along with exploitation and lack of recognition, are the plight of migrant workers. When it comes to women migrant labourers and children, the situation becomes more vulnerable.

In December 2015, three migrant labourers, totally exhausted, approached Jan Jagruti Kendra (JJK), a voluntary organisation in Pithora, Chhattisgarh, seeking help to get back family members who were struggling in a brick kiln in the state of Jammu and Kashmir. Eighty people (workers and their families) were taken from a village in the Janjir Chapa district of Chhattisgarh by a labour contractor from the same village after he paid a token advance amount. At the kiln, they had to work under exploitative conditions without wages and were forced to work for long hours without breaks. Even children and pregnant women were not spared; they too were forced to work to meet the targets set by the brick kiln owner. After three months of work, when a few of the workers expressed their desire to go back to the village to cast their vote for the panchayat elections, the employers not only denied them leave but started verbal abuse along with physical torture. However, Heera, Munna and Mukesh managed to run away and reach Chhattisgarh. They wanted their family to be released and hence sought the help of JJK. Through JJK's intervention, an order was issued by the government to raid the brick kilns. When the owner of the kilns came to know about this order, the entire group of workers were loaded in a truck and off-loaded 100 kilometres away. It was in winter, and the workers had no food or shelter or money. Some found nearby work eventually to make enough money to return.

The story of these 80 people is not a new phenomenon in the brick kiln industry. A large chunk of the work force that migrates from remote villages in search of employment ends up labouring in brick kilns. Poverty, drought, malnutrition, starvation, anaemia, caste and many other socio-economic issues force the workers to migrate.

Brick Kilns - A Major Source of Employment

The images associated with brick-making areas in India are that of dry barren landscapes with heaps of bricks, huge chimneys, wandering children, and tiny shacks where the brick-makers live. Sheds made of unfired bricks with plastic sheets or leaves on top, entrances without doors where one has to crawl in, these are the places where entire families of four or five live. The workers, to meet the targets set by their employers, have to work for hours continuously with no rest at all. Using open space for daily chores, depending on nearby tanks or rivers for water, forest for firewood, they often live in brick kilns to earn their meagre wages. With no schools in the vicinity, their children loiter until they become part of the family labour.

Orissa is considered a key state for the supply of migrant labour, and around 2.5 million workers migrate annually from the state. Twelve districts in Orissa are highly migration-prone. The Koraput-Balangir-Kalahandi (KBK) region, which is among the poorest regions in the country, is the most migrant-prone area, and many Oriya workers end up either as bonded labour or in bonded-like situations.

According to the statistics of the Central Pollution Control Board, Delhi, millions of migrant workers work with their families in the country's many brick kilns. Since brick making is seasonal and lasts for six months, the workers are brought in by contractors after getting paid an advance. Once they take this advance and leave their homes, their woes begin.

Pitabash Dharu from Kanut village, Orissa, has one acre of land on which he and his family (wife and two children) work. "We are very poor and do not have any work during the drought season. We get no water, no jobs and literally starve for many days," Dharu has been quoted quoted as saying. (See *Labour File*, Vol. 9, No. 1-2, January-April 2014, SM, Cover Story, "Brick Kiln Workers in India: Migrating into Bondage," pages 6-44). He saw people from his village going out to different states looking for jobs. He too decided to migrate. An agent from a nearby village, Ashok Mahapatra, helped him migrate to a brick kiln in Andhra Pradesh. Brick kiln employers prefer family labour; therefore, he, his wife and a relative went as a unit to work in the brick kilns. The agent handed over an advance of Rs (Rupees) 40,000, which was given to him by a brick kiln owner in the Nellore district of Andhra Pradesh. Since Daru's children were in school, he left them with in-laws so that they could continue their studies. "We left our house and children behind and migrated to a new place where we neither knew anybody nor understood the region's language. We toiled for more than 14 hours a day. When we fell sick, we could not avail of any medical facilities." Every week, the family was given Rs 500, calculated on a per-day basis, for their food and other expenses. At the end of the season, the employer gave them Rs 1,500 each for their travel to their villages. Dharu said the employer told them "there was nothing more to pay since everything was paid as advance and weekly expenses."

Thus, they went back home empty-handed, as do a majority of the migrants in brick kilns.

The situation in the state of Jharkhand, which has brick kilns in 22 out of a total 24 districts, puts new emphasis on the pathetic condition in which the migrants work. They work in a bondage-like situation throughout the season only to repay their advance, but they end up getting more and more in debt. They are subjected to exploitative labour conditions by middlemen, recruiters and employers. Without any social support, they face severe physical, social and economic hardships.

The Middlemen: Tentacles of the Octopus

The middlemen or agents lure large numbers of poor men and women from their villages promising better employment and decent wages.

Soon these villagers realise that they are being trapped in an exploitation that they cannot escape. The advance payment offered to the worker forces the worker to be stuck with one employer, come what may. Along with irregular payment, money is deducted from the wages toward the commission of the middlemen.

Many employers in the textile city of Coimbatore in South India prefer employing young girls. They are less troublesome, docile and vulnerable. An agent who brings in a young girl for work is paid Rs. 500 by the employer on the condition that she will not quit before six months. If she leaves before six months, the agent will have to pay Rs. 1000 to the company. The agent who recruited her therefore plays the role of guardian angel of the girl and make sure that she doesn't leave the job. At the same time, he makes sure that the girl is taken out of that job after six months so that he can supply her to another company and get another Rs. 500.

Worse is the situation of the girls who work under the sumangali scheme that was introduced in the textile mills of Tamil Nadu for providing employment for three years to young girls of marriageable age. The girls will be paid a bulk amount between Rs. 50,000 to 100,000, along with wages at the end of three years, which could be used for their marriage. The agents bring in young girls of 16 to 18 years old from remote villages such as in Tamil Nadu and Kerala.

The girls are provided with accommodation and food on the factory premises, where they work on continuous shifts. After three years of long working hours, poor accommodation, horrible food, verbal abuse, and, in some cases, sexual exploitation, these girls are sent back with a fraction of the payment they were initially promised.

The Caste and Identity Crisis

Indian society is not yet free from the clutches of the caste system, though some visible changes are seen in urban areas. One economic sector that is inflicted by caste and language is domestic work. Lower-caste families continue to work as bonded labour for upper-caste landlords. As domestic workers, they are only entitled to food and shelter. The entire family is supposedly 'taken care of' by the families that employ them. The children are taught at a very young age to serve and never to question.

"My name is Ayeesha Beewi and I am 38 years old," the domestic worker told me in an interview. "I had to take out my burqa, put vermilion on my forehead and change my name to Radha for getting work in Delhi."

Ayeesha is from a village in West Bengal. She migrated to Delhi 12 years ago. She tried getting a job but couldn't since she was a Muslim. At present she works for five households in Delhi.

A Brahmin (upper caste) family will most likely employ a Brahmin cook. A lower-caste woman is expected to clean the vessels, sweep and mop the floor, and wash clothes but when it comes to cooking, the upper-caste community still prefers to employ upper-caste cooks. Even in states that boast of high literacy, the majority of domestic workers are dalits, or tribals, and they are conveniently understood to 'prefer' certain jobs. Yet 'preference' for a certain kind of work is not theirs to express. Although women migrate in large numbers to work in Delhi as domestic maids, Muslims and lower castes are not preferred. The lower caste people, especially the Dooms, Chamars and Muslims, have the worst lot.

Migrants in India usually form a class of invisible workers, yet with a visible contribution. A middle class family's daily routine could run amuck if its domestic help doesn't turn up for a day. Domestic maids in metro areas are largely migrants. Unemployment, poverty, loss in crops, mortgaged land, siblings to be married, death, and sickness are some of the factors that force these workers to migrate to cities in search of jobs. Besides, lured by the city life, many young girls join the group with the idea of getting some quick money. They are brought in by relatives, neighbours or friends from the same religion, community or caste. They come in through placement agencies as well.

The cases mentioned in the beginning--those of Rakhi Badra and Munirathinam--are sadly not isolated incidents. Atrocities against migrant domestic workers are on the increase, especially with live-in maids. India has yet to ratify internationally accepted labour codes for its 20 million domestic migrant workers.

Labour migration in India is a complex phenomenon with great economic and social implications. In today's globalized world with the phenomenal increase in modes of communication and transportation, the movement of communities and people in search of a better living is steadily on the rise.

Giving visibility to the migrant workforce should be a top priority of the government's. Awareness should be created to make migrants realise their rights as workers and as migrant workers.

India, being a democratic nation, should ensure the voting rights of migrant workers in the general elections. During migration, if there is no place to leave the school-going child, workers are forced to discontinue the child's education and take him or her along with them. Thus the need for the creation of more child care centres with hostel facilities at the source states so children's education can be continued unhindered. At the destination state, workers should be allowed access to free medical treatment in government hospitals.

Trade unions and civil society organisations should take the initiative to organise these workers so that they can collectively stand for their rights. Any violation of the rights of workers or atrocities against them should be treated as priorities.

Urbanization and migration—two inter-related phenomena of economic development—have the potential to transform society for good or ill. Attention has to be paid to these phenomena, certainly with close to 50 per cent of India's population estimated to be living in urban areas by 2030.

CHAPTER SEVEN

Migrant Workers Struggle to Survive in China

By

Nancy Yan Xu

Editor/General Manager

U.S. Edition, Global Times, Chinese and English language versions

Zhao Xiaoyun, a 44-year-old nanny working in Beijing, was overjoyed at her upcoming Lunar New Year holiday reunion with her son and daughter, both migrant workers in a coastal city in southeastern China. She planned to spruce up the holiday dinner for the family – the biggest meal of the year – with the most lavish hometown dishes, which included honeycomb-shaped steamed oat noodles with dipping sauces, also known in Chinese as *Kao Lao Lao*, bean flour soup, mutton pot with Chinese yams, and more.

Going Out

"I'm capable of cooking all flour-related dishes, which I've learned since childhood," Zhao said in a proud tone. "But I have little knowledge of how to cook fish because I hadn't seen or eaten any fish until I came to Beijing a couple of years ago. It seldom rained in my home village. When it did rain, we took a bath in the rain. That's a luxury."

Zhao works as a nanny for a wealthy family in Chaoyang District of Beijing, earning 2,700 yuan ($450) a month with free meals and lodging, plus a "red envelop" at year's end. She is responsible for accompanying the grandmother of the family to send kids to school and cooking some of the family dishes. "It's an easy job. The housework here is almost nothing compared with what I did on the farm at my home village. Though some things remind me of my status, the family generally is very nice to me," she said.

Zhao came from a remote village in Yuan Qu County of Shanxi Province. The county is one of the old revolutionary bases of China, where the Communist Party of China established its branch office in 1927 – only six years after the Party's birth and 22 years before the founding of the People's Republic of China. And yet the county also has poor villages located in barren and dry mountainous areas, such as Zhao's home village. Shanxi Province, famous for its wheat, vinegar, coal as well as wealthy coal mine owners, has about 3.29 million rural residents below the national poverty line of 2,300 yuan annually, or $1.03 daily. It ranks ninth among China's provinces in the size of its share of the nation's 88 million poor.

To Zhao and her fellow villagers, being a migrant worker in a big city – or to use their term, "going out" – is not a choice, but a must. Cities offer them a living that is not necessarily easy, but it is at least much less tough than their barren land back home. Through the networking of town fellows, Zhao sent her daughter to work as a lamp worker and her son as an electric welder, both in the southwestern city of Dongguan, Guangdong Province. Half a year later, she followed the steps of her children and came to Beijing as a nanny, leaving her crippled husband to take care of the small plots of land assigned to the family.

"When I stood at the Tian'anmen Square for the first time in my life, I was thrilled. I can hardly believe that I've got a job at the capital of China! I hope that my daughter and son would soon find a job here so my family can stay together. I miss them so much," said Zhao.

Dream Life

Compared with Zhao, Wang Caixia, a 50-year-old janitor for a luxury apartment complex in Chaoyang District, has settled down in the capital of China. She has a pretty stable job with a janitorial service company, responsible for cleaning a 16-story-high residential apartment in the complex and dumping the trash. In addition to janitorial work, she collects dumped paper cartons and plastic bottles, and sells them to recycling stations for a little bonus income for the family.

Wang's husband works as an electric welder at a small exhibit production company, earning 3,000 yuan ($500) monthly. Their son, born in Beijing, attends a local middle school for migrant children, excelling academically in math and science and having a good chance of going to high school and college.

"We've been living in Beijing for 13 years, long enough to call it our second home town. I'm happy to see our life steadily improved over the years," said Wang.

Despite increasingly referring to Beijing as her "home", she goes back to her home village at least once a year to see her mother and her mother-in-law, both in their mid-70s, and often remits money to them. "Our mothers are too old to relocate here and to adjust to Beijing life," she said.

Wang came from Fangzhuang Village of Xiangcheng County, Henan Province. Different from Nanny Zhao's home town, Xiangcheng County, a 2,100-year-old historic county, is one of the fast-growing rural economies in the province. Among the 700,000 rural population of the county, about 260,000 have chosen to break free from their home and to "go out" to pursue a new life in urban areas. They earn a total gross income of 3 billion yuan ($500 million), or 11,000 yuan ($1,923) per person annually.

Wang recalled that neither she nor her husband had a stable job during the early years of their migrant life. Her husband used to work for a construction team specializing in building the metal frames for tall buildings in Beijing. This was 10 years ago. She eventually persuaded her husband to quit the uninsured, high-risk job in which any wrong step could send him falling from high to a bone-shattering and perhaps deadly end.

"At that time, our son was small and didn't have health insurance coverage either. We were newcomers without Beijing *hukou*, the residence permit. I can't describe to you how hard and painstaking it was to have my son vaccinated. Now I feel so relieved as we've left the pain behind and are moving on in the right direction." She said their 13-year-long residence has entitled them to enrolling their son in public schools in Beijing.

Wang rents a cramped studio apartment of 20 square meters (215 square feet) in the basement of an old residence building. It is within walking distance of the luxury apartment where she works. "Sometimes the apartment is very stuffy as it doesn't have a window, but we like it because of its convenient location and cheap rent," she said, adding that the rent in Beijing has been soaring "crazily", with an ordinary one-bedroom apartment renting as high as 4,000 yuan ($800).

"Owning an apartment in Beijing is a dream too unrealistic to me," Wang said. "But I do dream of having a better education and becoming more competitive in the job market." She said that she dropped out of middle school to help her parents with farm work. Some of her former co-workers passed the maternity nanny test and with a license earn monthly wages of 12,000 yuan ($2,000).

Quiet Survivalists

While a lot of media spotlight has been shed on dramatic labor incidents, such as a spate of migrant workers' attempted suicides, totaling 18 in 2010, at Foxconn, the Chinese manufacturer of iPhones and iPads, many of China's 278 million migrant workers are quiet survivalists like Zhao and Wang, who are easily content with the simple joys of their urban life.

Both Zhao and Wang, though not well-educated and not Internet savvy, said that they have a second-hand smartphone that enables them to go online and to stay connected with family members and friends through WeChat, a popular Chinese social media platform with numbers of users totaling 500 million. "I traded in my old mobile phone, which was good for nothing except making phone calls," Wang said.

"For the luxury apartment complex where I work, the property management company has a labor union that occasionally organizes weekend entertainment activities for its employees, but our janitorial service company has no labor-union 'benefits' except giving each of us an extra 100 yuan ($17) a year," Wang said. "But it's okay. There's a small neighborhood park in front of the luxury apartment complex. Whenever I am available in the evening, I go there and watch local retired people gathering and square dancing for exercise to Chinese folk music. That's quite a moment of peace and relaxation for me."

Migration is not a new issue in China. The world's most populous country has witnessed its farmers' migration to cities for at least three decades, unleashed by Deng Xiaoping's reform and opening-up policy enacted in December 1978. China's net migration rate from 1949 to 1985 was estimated to be 0.24 per 1,000 population, much lower than the world average of 1.84 per 1000 from 1950 to 1990. However, in the mid-1980s, the migration waves started to accelerate at breakneck speed, soaring from 8.9 million migrants in 1989 to 23.0 million in 1994.

Poverty and idleness are two major forces that drive farmers out from their home villages. China has boasted of an emerging middle class population--with a $9,000-to-$34,000 average annual household income—that topped 300 million by 2012. Yet China still has at least 88 million people stuck in rural squalor and living below the national poverty line of $1.03 daily. Forging a life in the city means an average income three times that of the countryside.

For many migrant workers, however, what drives them to cities is not poverty but idleness. As in Zhao's home village, the small plots of barren, mountainous land assigned to families do not require all family members to work on them all year long. Even those elderly people who are left behind in villages to take care of the land often kill time by playing Mahjong or cards.

Urban life is by no means easy, though. The national system of *Hukou*, or residence permits, designed for a 1950s planned economy, remains a shackle for migrant workers in gaining equal access to health, housing, children's education, and social services in cities. The pressure for an overhaul or abolition of the residence permit system is mounting, but no one expects it to be a task achievable within a short period of time. Many migrant workers, who stay in cities as long as Wang's family but do casual manual work, have no required documents to apply for temporary resident permits and end up sending their children back to home villages to attend schools or receive medical services whenever they fall ill.

Restive strugglers

Migrant life is seen in a somewhat different way by young, unmarried migrant workers aged 18 to 25. Zhao's son and daughter, both of whom work at factories in the city of Dongguan and requested anonymity, expressed mixed feelings toward their new urban life, using such words as "boring", "stressful" and "toilsome".

It is among this young age group that dramatic labor incidents usually arise and catch the public eye. Zhao's son and daughter, each with nine years of education, said it was still common for factory bosses to delay wages owed to workers. Though they had no personal experience participating in labor protests, they both said "Good thing!" to such protests and to the labor strikes of recent years. For example, at Specialty Medical Supplies, a U.S.-based manufacturer of alcohol swabs and plastic injection devices with factories in Beijing's suburbs, disgruntled Chinese workers held their American boss for hours at his office in 2013 to get the company to pay overdue wages. The company decided to relocate the plastic injection assembly line to India.

China's Labor Law and Labor Contract Law, enacted in 1995 and 2008 respectively, entitle workers to fair wages without excessive overtime plus the right to negotiate with management as a group. However, the deliberate violation of these guaranteed rights is not uncommon in migrant factories outside Beijing, and this is what leads to social unrest and labor action.

An emerging awareness of the need to protect labor rights has also driven more workers to seek legal aid for peaceful resolution of labor issues. "Migrant workers are fighting in court to get delayed regular wages from their bosses, and more recently, fighting for their workers' compensation and overtime pay," said attorney Tong Lihua, director of the Beijing Zhicheng Legal Assistance Center of Migrant Workers. The center helped more than 10,000 migrant workers resolve labor issues between 2005 and 2013, securing payments of over 117 million yuan ($19.5 million) in delayed wages, compensatory and punitive damages. Although all employers in Beijing are required by law to file employees' information within a certain period of time upon employment, they often only selectively do so, Tong said. Construction teams, which recruit many migrant workers, often deliberately leave much of their employment information unfiled, making contract-based legal resolution difficult.

Home Sweet Home

The issue of Chinese migration has recently come to a turning point. The ongoing economic downturn fuels the outbreaks of more labor disputes as workers become more worried that they may lose their jobs, or that their bosses may flee without paying wages. China's annual GDP growth rate is expected to slow brutally from 9.8 percent in 1995-2009 to 6.1 percent in 2016-2020. Inflation rates and trade figures are also suggestive of an insufficient level of demand, which has forced factories to suspend their production lines and to lay off workers.

As their expectations for wages and equality clash with harsh reality, some migrant workers are starting to think twice about their decision of "going out". As a result, in a reversal of the long-dominant flow of migrants from rural to urban areas, more migrant workers have begun returning to their home villages in recent years in the belief that they may have a better quality of life when closer to home.

Meanwhile, Zhao and Wang are getting accustomed to the hustle and bustle of urban life, and they increasingly refer to the city where they have shed much sweat and tears as "home". During her well-prepared Lunar New Year dinner, Zhao greeted her children by saying "Welcome home!" and she meant it.

CHAPTER EIGHT

Japan's Ethnic Koreans: "Good Koreans or Bad Koreans, Kill Them Both!"

By

Takehiko Kambayashi

Tokyo correspondent for the German Press Agency (DPA)

Tokyo - In early 2013, more than 100 people, mostly men, started to march through a crowded Korean neighborhood of central Tokyo. Almost every week, the marchers threatened violence and hurled slurs at Koreans, including children.

Many of the marchers were waving signs, some of which read "Kill all Koreans!" "Beat to death 50,000 Korean prostitutes!" and "Good Koreans or bad Koreans, kill them both!" Interestingly, some signs also showed support for nuclear energy. It was two years after Japan's worst nuclear disaster at the Fukushima Daiichi Nuclear Power Station in March 2011.

Major media first downplayed or ignored the hate speech. However, a growing number of citizens, activists and some lawmakers spoke out in defense of Koreans, often getting into a shouting match with the marchers on the streets. On several occasions, such quarrels escalated into fights and arrests were made.

It is yet another case of ethnic Koreans in Japan becoming targets of hatred and discrimination. The new anti-Korean group—called Zaitokukai, or Citizens Against the Special Privileges of Koreans in Japan--emerged amid North Korea's international provocations, missile launches and nuclear tests. There is also the long-stalled issue of Pyongyang's abductions of Japanese nationals in the 1970s and 1980s.

The emergence of the group came a few months after Prime Minister Shinzo Abe took office. Abe gained popularity by bashing North Korea and South Korea. Prior to the Korean War (1950 – 1953) that divided the peninsula, Korea was under Japanese colonial rule from 1910 to 1945. Critics say Japan's major media, which were struggling with falling ratings and circulation numbers in the Internet age, sensationalized North Korean threats and Japan's strained ties with South Korea.

With the number of ethnic Koreans in Japan at more than 500,000 as of December 2014, they are second only to the Chinese among the largest non-Japanese groups in the country, according to the Justice Ministry. The number does not include those naturalized in Japan. The country's census figures do not show ethnicity.

Many Koreans in Japan are second or third-generation immigrants, and they live across the country. They have grown up in Japan, and many of them don't even speak the Korean language. Still, these Japanese-born Koreans are not granted citizenship and not allowed to vote.

In early 2013, Education Minister Hakubun Shimomura decided to eliminate schools for ethnic Koreans from the Japanese government's tuition-waiver program due to the lack of progress on the abduction issue between Japan and North Korea. Korean school officials argued their students had nothing to do with issues between the two countries. Furthermore, more than 50 per cent of their students are citizens of South Korea, they said.

The minister's move came with the emergence of the Zaitokakai group. The year 2013 also marked the 90th anniversary of the massacre of thousands of ethnic Koreans in Tokyo and its surrounding areas after a major earthquake that struck the region on September 1, 1923, killing 105,000.

Soon after the Great Kanto Earthquake, historians say, military and police spread false information that ethnic Koreans had started riots, setting fires, throwing bombs and poisoning city wells. Koreans were hunted down and killed on the spot by the authorities and vigilante groups organized by citizens. Japanese socialists and ethnic Chinese were also murdered in the turmoil.

More than 6,000 people, most of them Koreans, were killed, according to historians and activists. Still, the Japanese government has never acknowledged that the massacre took place.

"If the government had conducted a thorough investigation into the massacre 90 years ago and carried out substantive countermeasures, we would not see the hate speech today," said Masao Nishizaki, a leader of a Tokyo-based citizens group that has investigated the killing. "The Japanese government bears grave responsibility. There may have been some investigation, but its findings were never made public." [1]

Nishisaki's group, one of several support/advocacy groups active on behalf of Koreans in Japan, calls itself *Hosenka*, Japanese for jewelweed, or the rather long name of The Association for Recovering the Remains of Koreans Slaughtered soon after the Kanto Great Earthquake and Commemorating Them.

The 1923 massacre took place at a time when an increasing number of Koreans came to Japan to seek jobs because of the hardships they faced in Korea under Japanese colonial rule. The number of Koreans in Japan grew from 37,732 in 1919 to 136,557 in 1923, according to Shoji Yamada, a historian and professor emeritus at Rikkyo University in Tokyo. [2]

The immigration benefited companies in Japan that wanted cheap labor to survive tough economic times and thus started to replace unskilled Japanese workers with newly-arrived Koreans.

Under such circumstances, increasing numbers of unskilled Japanese workers felt antipathy toward Korean workers, Yamada says in his book *Kanto daishinsai ji no chosenjin gyakusatsu to sonogo*. [3]

Nishizaki's Hosenka was established in 1982 with the challenge to find the remains of the victims in the little-known tragedy. Early on they dug in areas on the bank of Arakawa River in downtown Tokyo, where some killings were believed to have taken place in 1923, but they were not able to locate any remains.

The group later found newspaper articles from 1923 which showed that, two months after the massacre, the military dug up the remains of the victims and carried them away as police cordoned off areas along the bank to keep onlookers out.

"When the police came to realize there had been no riot by Koreans, they concocted an uprising led by Koreans, refused to hand over the remains of the victims and hid them in order to cover up the reality of the massacre," Yamada says. "They also clamped down on gatherings by Koreans to mourn the victims." [4]

Nishizaki, a former public school teacher, spent four years combing through tens of thousands of books at dozens of libraries in Tokyo and neighboring areas and compiled witness accounts into three booklets.

"That's all we can do now at this point. It is very frustrating," he said. Of the more than 6,000 victims, only the names of 70 to 80 people are recorded. [5]

Every September since 1982, his group, along with locals and ethnic Koreans, holds a memorial service on the banks of Arakawa River for the thousands of nameless victims.

"We don't know exactly whom we are commemorating," Nishizaki said.

The group decided to build up a monument near the bank to commemorate the victims since they could not find any remains. Local government, however, refused to cooperate with the group. Local leaders said there is no public record that gives proof of the massacre, even though a pile of such public documents were submitted to them, Nishizaki told me. It appears local government cannot concede what the central government has never acknowledged. [6]

The monument was finally erected in 2009 after the group collected donations.

Kang Duk Sang, professor emeritus of contemporary Korean history at the University of Shiga Prefecture, argued in a 2013 speech that "without the institution of martial law, the massacre would not have happened. Under martial law, the Japanese military had effectively seized power." [7]

Japan had never declared a state of martial law unless there was war or an insurgency, Kang said. Who caused an insurgency then? Groundless rumors circulated by authorities claimed it was ethnic Koreans.

"It is Rentaro Mizuno [who then served as Interior Minister] who said clearly 'The enemy is Koreans,'" Kang said. "At around 10 a.m. on September 2 [in 1923], police also started saying, 'It's okay to kill Koreans.'" September 2 was the day following the quake. [8]

Experts and activists are beginning to shed light on the massacre. However, many Japanese are still unaware of the mass killing and the government's responsibility because schools and the country's mainstream media fail to discuss it.

Nishizaki told me the massacre is not a thing of the past as victims' families have been waiting to recover the remains for several generations, and they are still in pain even after 90 years.

When Nishizaki made a speech on the issue in front of Korean lawmakers and citizens in Seoul a few years ago, one elderly man approached him at the event and said that his grandfather's name was not on the list of the victims. The man asked him to look for remains of the grandfather. [9]

A growing number of citizens, activists and scholars want the Japanese government to be held responsible for the massacre and the subsequent failure to investigate it. They collected signatures and submitted them to parliament in 2014.

* * *

At a posh café in a tony district of Tokyo, Lee Son Ja, a second-generation of Korean in Tokyo, told me how her father Lee In Seop survived the massacre.

The soft-spoken vocal instructor said her father had no choice in coming to Japan in his 20s, just like many ethnic Koreans at that time, because of the hardships of life in the homeland after Japan occupied the Korean Peninsula in 1919. Upon his arrival in Kawasaki city, south of Tokyo, he toiled long hours for a poorly paying job at a port. [10]

Following the devastating quake in 1923, a Japanese boss rushed to his employees, saying some people told him that a group of Koreans were on the way to kill all Japanese. Lee's father tried to get the fearful Japanese calmed down, saying he would talk the Koreans out of it if they indeed came. After a while, the boss came rushing over to the father again, saying this time he heard all Koreans were going to be killed.

The boss put the Korean in a closet to harbor him. After four days, as violence against Koreans intensified, the boss decided to let him get on a ship that was about to leave the port. He did not know the ship was bound for the northern island of Hokkaido, more than 600 miles away from Tokyo. This is where he started a new life, and where Lee and her six siblings grew up. [11]

Lee's father survived the mass killing, but struggles continued even after arriving on the island. "My father was a very hard-working man. At that time, it was very difficult for even Japanese people to find a job on Hokkaido. He went wherever there was a job, so every one of our seven siblings was born in a different place." [12]

Most of the time, Lee's father worked as a construction worker. However, he also worked at a mine for a time and was involved in a cave-in that cost him one eye and most of his eyesight in the other. He and his wife started a cheap lodging house near the mine, where Lee saw American and European prisoners of war who appeared to have been forcibly brought in to work deep in the mountains during World War II. [13]

Lee's father died at the age of 50. The family lost the inn and moved to the port city of Otaru, where her mother found work as a dock laborer to raise her seven children. Lee came to Tokyo to seek a job after graduating from high school on the island. She later attended a college of music to become a vocal instructor.

Lee is married to a Korean man who runs a company in Tokyo. They have two daughters and one grandchild. The younger one is a professional singer who just held two sold-out concerts with large audiences.

Lee said she has been supported by many Japanese, but she still faces discrimination because of her ethnicity. "It's very complicated," she said.

She participates in a memorial of the massacre every year and sings songs in memory of her father and the victims.

Lee told me she and her siblings are grateful to the quick-thinking Japanese boss, whose name they don't know.

"It was the Japanese boss who saved my father's life. If my father had been killed, we would not be here." [14]

Joseph B. Atkins, Professor of Journalism, University of Mississippi, USA.

CHAPTER NINE

Singapore: Citadel of Neoliberalism

By

Joseph B. Atkins

Professor of Journalism, University of Mississippi, USA

SINGAPORE – W. Somerset Maugham, this city's most famous expatriate writer, once had this to say about Southeast Asia's peasant workers:

"These patient, industrious folk carry on the same yokes the same burdens as their ancestors carried so many generations back. The centuries have passed leaving no trace upon them. … In these countries of the East the most impressive, the most awe-inspiring monument of antiquity is neither temple, nor citadel, not great wall, but man. The peasant with his immemorial usages belongs to an age far more ancient than Angkor Wat, the Great Wall of China, or the Pyramids of Egypt." [1]

Maugham was much on my mind when I traveled to Singapore a few years ago. I wanted to sit in the Long Bar at the Raffles Hotel, a Gin Pahit in one hand and Maugham's *The Gentleman in the Parlour* in the other.

I knew better but I imagined a Singapore like Maugham experienced in the 1920s, or what Bob Owens, a retired Navy friend of mine in Memphis who was there in the late 1940s, called a "flat, sprawling Asian city" of temples, bordellos, colonial government buildings, and shacks.

Of course, what I found was an ultra-modern Singapore of monster skyscrapers that completely dwarf what remains of the old city--the Raffles, the 170-year-old Cathedral of the Good Shepherd, the shophouses in Chinatown. The sleepy-but-exotic port-of-call my friend Bob saw is today a dynamic crossroads of Asian and Western cultures, an economic powerhouse that is a model to the rest of southeast Asia, a city-state that *The Economist* calls the "least corrupt and best place to do business in the world," better than the United States, Switzerland, and even perennial rival Hong Kong. [2]

Still, Maugham's words about the Asian peasant are as true today as they were when he wrote them in 1930. Singapore would still be a Third World backwater if it weren't for the legions of migrant workers from Bangladesh, India, Malaysia, Indonesia, the Philippines, and China who do the backbreaking work to make it a thriving neoliberal citadel.

One in 20 Singaporeans will be a millionaire by 2017, projects a study cited in the British newspaper *The Guardian*. [3] Yet more than one-third of the workforce in this city of 5.5 million is foreign-born, and many of them live in crowded, rat-infested dormitories with little relief from the sweltering tropical heat, reliving the conditions that faced the 19th century immigrants from China who largely built Singapore. The descendants of those Chinese as well as Malay and Indian Singaporeans make up the native population.

"Singapore may be seen by some as a model in ways that are not so good for workers," said John Gee, a prominent migrant worker advocate and former president of the Singapore-based Transient Workers Count Too (TWC2) organization. "It has made some reforms, shown a real commitment to countering the worst abuses of workers, but this still leaves a long way to go. We'd like to see a new relationship worked out." [4]

Many Singaporeans have no idea of the horrible housing conditions and other abuses that migrant workers suffer, Gee said. [5]

There's no minimum wage in the most expensive city in the world. Union representation is rare among migrant workers, and they're forbidden to demonstrate publicly. Workers' compensation for injuries on the job is a long, tortuous process that may or may not bring relief and could result in deportation. A migrant worker from Bangladesh told *The Daily Beast* in 2013 his employer refused to help him with his extensive hospital bills after he suffered a disabling injury on his construction job. "I was very good," he told reporter Kirsten Han, "but now I have an accident, I'm no good." [6]

Most migrant workers live in Third World conditions, earning as low as 2 Singapore dollars (S$2), or $1.60 (U.S.), per hour. [7] Overall wages for many wage earners in Singapore actually declined between 1998 and 2008, leaving those workers with less purchasing power than the citizens of nearby Kuala Lumpur, Malaysia. Yet, with unemployment rates as little as under 2 percent, immigration doubled in the first decade of the new century.

Migrant workers are mired in debt on the day they arrive on the shores of Singapore. They owe so much to training centers back home, recruiters and agents that they may have to work up to three years just to recoup the money they spent to get to Singapore. This accrued indebtedness as well as the subsequent substandard living and working conditions are the result of "an intricate web of deals, kickbacks, dodgy contracts, exploitation and abuse," wrote Kirsten Han in *The Daily Beast*. [8]

This is ironic given Singapore's reputation as "the least corrupt ... place to do business in the world." Its politicians are the world's highest paid. The high pay—Singapore's prime minister earns five times as much as a U.S. president—has been touted as a means to keep out corruption. Although public disgruntlement and the recommendations of a 2011 independent review committee led to a 36 percent pay cut for politicians in recent years, Singaporean politicians' salaries remain the envy of their peers around the globe.

In 2010, Singapore emerged from its worst recession in history by registering 15.5 percent growth in the first quarter of that year. [9] Manufacturing, 25 percent of the economy and led by the electronics and biomedical industries, jumped 32.9 percent. [10] Its growth has continued. The city's skyline rivals those of Chicago and Hong Kong, and it now includes the $7.8 billion, 55-story three towers of the Marina Bay Sands luxury hotel and casino with their connecting 2,500-acre sky terrace. Long one of the Pacific Rim's economic "tigers," the city pulses with energy from its financial district down to its busy ethnic enclaves with their Buddhist and Hindu temples, Moslem mosques, and vendor and shophouse-lined streets.

Yet this financial powerhouse reserves most of its rewards for those at the top end of the economy. The wealthy pay just half in taxes what their counterparts in the United States pay. Already-low corporate taxes were cut even lower during the 2009 recession. Sales taxes, on the other hand, rose from 4 percent in 2003 to 7 percent.

"The government keeps raising (sales) taxes, putting pressure on people, particularly small businessmen," a convenience store owner in western Singapore complained to me during my visit. "You have to work very hard to make it. You have to get up early and go to bed late. People are scared to speak up. Even the rich are scared to say anything or they will lose what they have." [11]

Ang Peng Hwa, director of the Singapore Internet Research Centre at Singapore's Nanyang Technological University, said the influx of immigrant workers has kept wages low while "the differential between the wealthy and the poor is growing." [12]

Workers have no real means to protest their conditions. Under the semi-authoritarian, half-century rule of the People's Action Party and, for much of that time, the watchful eye of modern Singapore's late founder and *minister mentor*, Lee Kuan Yew, any kind of protest has been strictly limited.

Remember this is the city where American Michael Fay was famously caned for theft and vandalism in 1994. The Singapore Police are notoriously tough. No jaywalking, and no eating and drinking in the subways. Graffiti artists face up to three years in prison--plus the cane--if they get caught.

"Outdoor protests of the kind we see in the rest of the world are largely banned," said Radha Basu, a senior correspondent with *The Straights Times*, Singapore's major newspaper, and a frequent writer about migrant worker issues. "Impoverished migrant workers who are desperate to remain in Singapore to earn decent salaries don't generally protest (although) there have been cases where groups have thronged (Ministry of Manpower) headquarters to complain about non-payment of salaries." [13]

Basu's reportage has helped bring attention to migrant workers' plight. Her articles in 2010 on their poor housing conditions may have helped prompt a subsequent crackdown by the government on some of the city's worst slum lords. She described worker dormitories where rats and cockroaches freely scurried across rooms, kitchens "mired in grime" with overflowing sinks and debris everywhere. "Cooking here makes me want to vomit," migrant construction worker V. Ramamoorthy, a native of India, told her. [14]

Gee said workers should be able "to speak up for their own rights without fear of being sent home by their employers in order to shut them up and frighten others. That would make Singapore into a much better model to follow." [15]

Long-simmering frustration among Singapore's migrant workers exploded in December 2013 after a worker died in a bus accident in the city's Little India section. An estimated 400 people set fire to vehicles, threw stones, and attacked city emergency personnel who had come to the scene. It was the worst—and only —major riot in Singapore since 1969. In 2012, Chinese bus drivers protested wages that were lower than those paid native and Malay drivers. Bangladeshi workers also protested, but the reason for their protest was they weren't paid at all.

The government has little tolerance for such disruptions. Prime Minister Lee Hsien Loong called the riot in Little India an "isolated incident" caused by an "unruly mob." [16] Dozens were arrested in that incident and faced criminal charges.

Singapore celebrated the 50th anniversary of its independence from Malaysia in 2015, and many Singaporeans credit the late Lee Kuan Yew for raising the city from Third World to First World status. Lee died in March 2015 at the age of 91 after guiding the city-state as prime minister and later as *minister mentor*. The current prime minister, Lee Hsien Loong, is his son.

"Lots of foreigners come here to work," 55-year-old taxi driver Abo Rhaman B Abo Samad told me during my visit. "Everybody has a job if you're not too choosy. I was a security guard making eight hundred to nine hundred (Singapore) dollars salary. I had to upgrade myself. Now I make four thousand a month."

Lee Kuan Yew was "a smart man, a swell leader, a great leader. We have nothing, no natural resources. This man took us out of nothing." Lee's critics "are stupid. They haven't been to Myanmar (Burma), or to Thailand where they are fighting." [17]

Indeed, over the two weeks I spent in Singapore back in 2010, the streets of Bangkok turned red with blood as Red Shirt protesters raged against the government. North and South Korea rattled sabers over the sinking of a South Korean warship. Worker suicides and bizarre attacks on children and women revealed the dark underside to China's economic boom. Indonesian police raided a terrorist hideout in Jakarta and found plans indicating that one of the subway stops I used everyday in Singapore was a bombing target.

Meanwhile, growing unrest among workers in China, India, and other countries was watched closely in Singapore. Nearly 2,000 workers for Honda in China's Guangdong province went on strike in mid-May that year, shutting down production at the company's four plants there. They were protesting low wages and poor working conditions. Workers at the Hyundai plant in Chennai, India, shut down operations there, too, in June. A rash of suicides by workers at Foxconn Technology's plants in Shenzhen, China, prompted the company to raise wages twice within a single week —first by 30 percent, and then by 70 percent. Foxconn makes electronic components for Dell, Apple and other companies, including Apple's iPhone and iPad.

At the time of Lee Kuan Yew's death in March 2015, Singapore still sat "in a region rife with political instability and corruption," according to *The Economist*. [18] Malaysia Prime Minister Najib Razak's administration was mired in scandal and debt as a result of misspent investment funds as well as political controversy over the government's hounding of political opponents and its new Prevention of Terrorism Act, allowing indefinite detentions of suspects without trial. Singapore even found its reputation for clean, pollution-free air tarnished in June 2013 after a haze descended on the city that forced citizens to don face masks when they went outdoors. The cause? Forest burning in Indonesia.

As activist Gee said, Singapore has tried to address worker concerns. In March 2012, Minister of State for Manpower Tan Chuan Jin announced that domestic workers in Singapore would get a compulsory day of rest. The number of foreign domestic workers grew from 140,000 in 2002 to 201,000 by 2010. [19] For each year from 2012 to 2015, the joint government-private sector National Wages Council proposed raises for low-wage workers to get them over a S$1,100 threshold. However, less than one-third of companies complied with the council's call for a S$60 hike in 2014. The city has also taken some action to improve workers' living conditions, moving close to 20,000 in 2009 to better facilities and increasing inspections. Fines against slumlords officially can be as high as $5,000 plus six months in jail, but in reality fines often have been as little as 200 Singapore dollars.

"Employers are responsible for the upkeep and maintenance of their foreign workers, including the provision of acceptable accommodation," Joann Tan, a spokeswoman with Singapore's Ministry of Manpower (MOM), told me. [20]

The city-state's Ministry of Manpower reported in 2012 that it had taken action against nearly 8,000 employers since 2005 for failing to provide adequate housing to workers.

These government responses to migrant workers' plight can be in part attributed to various organizations working on their behalf and providing them a voice in public discourse. At the forefront has been the nonprofit Transient Workers Count Too (TWC2), providing food programs, a hotline, research, and other direct services. Dozens of volunteers help migrant workers resolve work-related problems, make hospital appointments, and get good meals. The organization gets up to 200 new cases—many of them wage and compensation complaints or health-related issues--each month and usually is dealing with as many as 500 at a time. [21] After TWC2 discovered that the Minister of Manpower was taking more than two years to resolve cases involving male workers, the ministry responded by speeding up the process and now "the great majority of cases are resolved within a year," Gee said. [22]

Nevertheless, and despite the city's long history of immigration, a backlash against migrant workers is growing among the native population. Native Singaporeans resent blue-collar immigrants for keeping wages low, and they resent white-collar immigrants for taking away jobs. "Some quite venomous anti-migrant worker statements may be heard in casual conversation," Gee said. "It is easy politics all over the world: blame the foreigner. None of the opposition parties speak up for them, as they see that as a vote loser." [23]

Journalist Radha Basu agreed. "Foreign workers in Singapore are increasingly being blamed for all kinds of ills—from low wages to (the) crowded transport system to soaring property taxes and even petty crime." [24]

Thousands of Singaporeans critical of immigration protested in early 2013 after a published report indicated government support for a projected 30 percent growth in the country's population by 2030 with migrants constituting half that growth.

Public criticism frequently points at the behavior and cultural idiosyncrasies of foreigners. A Chinese migrant family's formal complaint about the unpleasant smell of curry prepared by local neighbors in 2011 led to a furious Facebook battle with nearly 60,000 natives supporting a special "curry" Sunday in which everyone prepared curry. [25]

Yet, Gee said, "the construction sector would grind to a halt without migrant workers; likewise, the shipyard sector. Probably cleaning services would be badly hit, too. Migrant workers provide a substantial minority of the workforce who drive buses, work in shops and restaurants. One in six households have domestic workers. ... Despite lots of complaints by sectors of the public about the presence of foreign workers, most people know that if they were excluded tomorrow, it would be catastrophic for the national economy." [26]

In other words, the peasant worker still has "his immemorial usages," and he still builds the citadels, but he remains as anonymous and unappreciated as his ancestors.

POSTSCRIPT:

The Immigrants' Tango in Argentina

By Joseph B. Atkins

Professor of Journalism, University of Mississippi, USA

BUENOS AIRES, Argentina – We're in the century-old Confitería Ideal listening to the mother of all tangos, "La Cumparsita", and I'm thinking about the crime and poverty-ridden barrio world into which the tango was born. Argentine writer Jorge Luis Borges describes it perfectly in his short story, "Streetcorner Man".

"He was admired for the way he handled a knife," Borges says about the Slasher, a barrio gang leader in his story. "Sharp dresser, too. He always rode up to the whorehouse on a dark horse, his riding gear decked out in silver. ... He usually wore a soft hat with a narrow brim ... it would sit in a cocky way on his long hair, which he slicked straight back."

Then one night the Slasher's rival—whom they called the Butcher—challenged him for his woman. "He called to the musicians to play loud and strong, and he ordered the rest of us to dance. From one end of the hall to the other, the music ran like wildfire. ... `Make way, boys, she's all mine now!'"

The tango was the music of Argentina's poor creole natives and its immigrants, Italians mostly, who came by the millions to Argentina in the late 1800s. The music was sad, sometimes angry, often fatalistic, reflecting homesickness, resentment against the "patrón", or despair for the woman who had made their lives hell. They spoke a distinct dialect, lunfardo, the language of some of the greatest tangos.

The immigrants came as a result of the governing elite's "gobernar es poblar" ("to govern is to populate") policy at the turn of the last century, a policy to import cheap European labor to work the newly cultivated fields in Argentina's vast countryside as well as in its urban ports and construction sites, and also to lift the country beyond the creole culture that was seen as a hindrance to progress.

As "wealth … was routed to Buenos Aires and to Europe, it was thus confirmed that tenancy, sharecropping, and land speculation would be the agricultural destiny of Argentina," Robert D. Crassweller writes in his monumental *Perón and the Enigmas of Argentina*. As for the city, "many immigrants, in fact, never penetrated beyond the capital."

Thus, the creole and the immigrant were pitted against one another, not only in competition for work but also Argentina's soul. The tango, created by the creole and adopted by the immigrant, reflected a world disconcerting to both, a strange, dark, unfamiliar world where the deck seemed stacked against them. Out of their struggle came the nation's greatest art form and gift to the rest of the world.

"The pervasive sense of sadness (in the tango) is tied to the immigrant as a physical presence of the elite's destruction of creole Argentina," writes Donald S. Castro in his 1991 book *The Argentine Tango As Social History (1880-1955): The Soul of the People*. "Both the immigrant and the creole made the tango their vehicle for expressing their feelings."

Castro quotes the writer Ernesto Sábato to explain further: "'It was as painful for the immigrant to hear the creole bitterness, as it was for the creole to see his country invaded by strangers.'"

The dance, sensuous beyond all other dances, tells of the importance of women in their lives. Women were greatly outnumbered in those Wild West years of Argentina, and when a man got one on the floor, he held her close, cheek to cheek, and his sharp, lunging steps were like the wave of a stiletto, a warning to other men to stay away.

Unlike in the United States where politicians from presidential candidate Donald Trump to Mississippi Governor Phil Bryant seem to have forgotten their own immigrant ancestry and demagogue the modern-day immigrant as the "other", a source of endless problems, Argentina has a deep consciousness of its immigrant heritage. By 1914, 58 percent of Argentines were first or second generation immigrants. Seventy percent of Buenos Aires' population was foreign-born. They were important in

Argentina's rise to one of the world's sixth richest countries by 1920.

Argentina's most famous military leaders, politicians and artists—from José de San Martín and Juan Perón to writer Borges and tango crooner Carlos Gardel—were either immigrants or exiles during their lifetimes. "Deep down, (Astor) Piazzolla himself was always something of an uprooted, nostalgic migrant," María Susana Azzi and Simon Collier write in their biography of the prominent master of so-called "Nuevo Tango", who spent formative years in New York City.

At a time when Republican politicians in the United States were demanding a ban on Syrian immigrants and a wall between the nation's southern border and Mexico, Argentina boasted one of the world's most open policies toward immigration. Laws were passed in 2004 and 2013 guaranteeing equality and workplace protection to such workers as the country's 100,000 Paraguayan domestic workers. They get maternity leave, paid holidays, and they cannot be forced to work more than 48 hours a week.

As we've seen throughout this book, migrants are a global phenomenon. Between 2000 and 2010, their number grew from 150 million to 214 million. Add war and political strife to economic pressures—such as in Syria, Libya, and elsewhere across the troubled world--and you've got huge portions of the global population in a constant search for a better life. Exacerbating those economic pressures are neoliberal policies that exploit cheap migrant work through trade agreements like NAFTA and the Trans-Pacific Partnership (TPP). These agreements may enrich hedge fund operators on Wall Street and fatten the coffers of the politicians who support them but they usually bring nothing but misery to working people.

Argentina was an early victim of neoliberalism and its insistence on deregulation, privatization, free market globalization, and crushing foreign indebtedness, factors that plunged the nation into bankruptcy and depression in 2001. The economic crisis led to the out-migration of hundreds of thousands of Argentines of European descent in search of a better life abroad. Ironically, the nation continued to lure low-wage, unskilled workers from neighboring countries in South America.

One of the most amazing stories to come out of Argentina's economic struggles is told in *Sin Patrón*, a book by the Lavaca Collective (a worker-run collective of journalists in Argentina). It recounts how workers themselves took over approximately 170 once-productive companies that had gone into bankruptcy as a result of business practices that had saddled them with enormous debt while enriching corporate executives.

The economy recovered greatly over the course of 12 years (2004-2015) of pro-worker, left-leaning Peronist rule by the late Néstor Kirchner and his wife Cristina. However, elections in 2015 put wealthy neoliberal Mauricio Macri into the presidency and signaled a shift back to the principles that earlier had Argentina on the rack and more recently Greece.

The great tango poet and lyricist Enrique Santos Discépolo offered the tanguero's classic cynical view of how money and greed can undermine the lives of both the native and the immigrant.

> *Don't you see, you poor fool*
> *That whoever's got the most dough is right?*
> *That honor's sold for cash, and morals for pennies?*
> *That no truth can withstand two bucks*

Just as they did at the turn of the last century, native workers in Argentina worry that Macri may turn the immigration issue against them by opening the floodgates to cheap, non-organized foreign workers from Bolivia and other countries. "How do you care for Argentine workers if you open the doors like what was done in the 1990s?" Hernan Pose, a member of the CTA (Central de trabajadores de la Argentina) workers organization, told me as he handed out anti-Macri leaflets in Buenos Aires' busy Calle Florida in November 2015.

His colleague and fellow CTA member Rodolfo Olmos nodded. "Yes, it is a big problem."

So even with its rich immigrant tradition and welcoming policies, Argentina isn't immune to tensions over migrant workers. Let's hope its politicians don't look northward toward that big behemoth beyond the Rio Grande for a model in how to handle those tensions. Let's hope it remains a beacon of light—much like the workers and worker organizations in Florida, Israel, Hong Kong, Singapore and beyond you've encountered in this book—in the fight over migrant worker rights.

We all need beacons of light for together they become a field of energy—a movement, if you will—with all the potential necessary to dispel the darkness others want to impose.

Perhaps the best advice comes from that great Argentine, former Buenos Aires Archbishop Jorge Mario Bergoglio, better known today as Pope Francis. "Thousands of persons are led to travel north in search of a better life," he told the U.S. Congress in September 2015. "We must not be taken aback by their numbers but rather view them as persons, seeing their faces and listening to their stories, trying to respond as best we can to their situation. To respond in a way which is always humane, just and fraternal."

NOTES

INTRODUCTION

1 Vietnamese migrant worker, interview by author, Bade City, Taiwan, 15 March 2011.

2 Father Peter Nguyen Hung Cuong, interview by author, Bade City, Taiwan, 15 March 2011.

3 Diego Reyes Sr., interview by author, Sanford, N.C., 3 July 2010.

4 Southern Poverty Law Center, *Close to Slavery: Guestworker Programs in the United States* (Montgomery, Ala.: SPLC), 2, 42.

5 Diego Reyes Jr., interview by author, Sanford, N.C., 3 July 2010.

6 John Gee, e-mail interview by author, e-mail, 20 June 2010.

7 Mariane Carnate, interview by author, Hong Kong, 2 June 2013.

8 David Bacon, *Illegal People* (Boston: Beacon Press, 2008), 73.

9 Bacon, *Illegal People*, 75, 76.

10 David Bacon, "Migration: A Product of Free Market Reforms," Americas Program website (posted December 1, 2012). See http://www.cipamericas.org/archives/6038.

11 The Rev. Carlton Eversley, interview by author, telephone, 26 June 2010.

12 Jennifer Gordon, "Citizens of the Global Economy," *New Labor Forum* 20 (Winter 2011): 57-64.

13 Nelva Baldon, interview by author, Taipei, Taiwan, 13 March 2011.

14 Sheila Z. Mayanoia, interview by author, Taipei, Taiwan, 13 March 2011.

15 Sister Eulalia P. Loreto, interview by author, Taipei, Taiwan, 18 March 2011.

16 Cynthia Ca Abdon-Tellez, interview by author, Hong Kong, 5 June 2013.

17 Reyes Jr., interview.

18 Reyes Jr., interview.

19 Sandy Smith-Nonini, "A Union Is the Only Way," *Southern Exposure* (summer 1999): 47.

20 Silvia Giagnoni, *Fields of Resistance: The Struggle of Florida's Farmworkers for Justice* (Chicago: Haymarket Books, 2011), 41.

21 Alexandria Jones, interview by author, Winston-Salem, N.C., 2 July 2010.

22 Rita Olivia Tambunan, "A Living Wage for Asian Garment Workers," *International Union Rights* 18 (2011): 20-21.

CHAPTER TWO

1 This essay is an adapted, expanded version of the speech I was invited to give at Springboard the annual fundraiser of the Civic Media Center in Gainesville, Florida, in March of 2013. I also wish to thank Sean Sellers, senior investigator with the Fair Food Standards Council, for helping me with the revision of this piece.

2 In February 2015, the CIW was awarded the Presidential Medal for Extraordinary Efforts to Combat Trafficking in Persons.

3 This quote is from http://www.fairfoodprogram.org. The list of the participating growers is updated and posted weekly on the Fair

Food Program website. Starting in June 2015, the FFP formally began expansion beyond Florida. The FFP will also be auditing farms in Georgia, North and South Carolina, Virginia and New Jersey. The recent farmworker-led Milk with Dignity campaign has been modeled after the CIW strategies. http://www.labornotes.org/2015/07/how-migrant-farmworkers-are-cross-pollinating-strategies-and-winning

4 Following the landmark agreement with the Florida Tomato Growers Exchange, the CIW begun using the "It's a New Day" slogan/chant.

5 A watershed moment was when the Florida Tomato Growers Exchange, which represents 90 percent of the state's farms, agreed to the CIW conditions and signed a historic agreement in 2010. The FTGE had earlier threatened its members with sanctions if they decided to comply with the "penny-per-pound" tomato program. The FTGE also had drafted a so-called New Social Responsibility Program, but it didn't meet the Coalition's standards as the code of conduct lacked worker participation.

6 Here is the complete list of the buyers that are now participating in the Fair Food Program: Yum Brands (2005), McDonald's (2007), Burger King (2008), Whole Foods Market (2008), Subway (2008), Bon Appetit Management Company (2009), Compass Group (2009), Aramark (2010), Sodexo (2010), Trader Joe's (2012), Chipotle Mexican Grill (2012), Walmart (2014), and Fresh Market (2015).

7 For a detailed account of the story, see the section "The King Is under the Table: Chronicle of a Victory Foretold" (208-211) in *Fields of Resistance: The Struggle of Florida's Farmworkers for Justice* (Haymarket Books, 2011) by Silvia Giagnoni.

CHAPTER FOUR

1 British nationals, Commonwealth citizens, and more recently EU nationals, were also permitted to apply for social housing, but the Moroccans

2 JC Culatto 'Things are a lot better for Moroccans in Gibraltar', *Panorama*, 9 November 2015

3 Sussex University Migration Briefing (December 2004)

4 See G Tremlett,. 'Rock and a Hard Place', *The Guardian*, 28 March 2009.

5 *Gibraltar Chronicle*, 30 March 2009.

6 G Tremlett,. 'Rock and a Hard Place', *The Guardian*, 28 March 2009.

7 D Blackburn, K Ewing and J Jeffries, 'Gibraltar's Treatment of Migrant Workers', *The Guardian*, 12 March 2009.

8 See G Tremlett,. 'Rock and a Hard Place', *The Guardian*, 28 March 2009.

9 See G Tremlett,. 'Rock and a Hard Place', *The Guardian*, 28 March 2009.

10 Vox Online, 9 April 2009.

11 HC 557 (2008-09)

12 Schengen visas cover most of the European Union but do not normally grant entry to the UK and Gibraltar, which are outside the Schengen area.

13 JC Culatto 'Things are a lot better for Moroccans in Gibraltar', *Panorama*, 9 November 2015

CHAPTER EIGHT

1 Masao Nishizaki, interview by author, Tokyo, Japan, 12 September 2013.

2 Shoji Yamada, *Kanto daishinsai ji no chosenjin gyakusatsu to sonogo* (Tokyo: Soushisha 2011) 20.

3 Yamada, *Kanto daishinsai ji no chosenjin gyakusatsu to sonogo*, 28.

4 Yamada, *Kanto daishinsai ji no chosenjin gyakusatsu to sonogo*, 13.

5 Nishizaki, interview.

6 Nishizaki, interview

7 Kang Duk Sang, speech at the History Museum of J-Koreans, 14 September 2013.

8 Kang, speech.

9 Nishizaki, interview.

10 Lee Son Ja, interview by author, Tokyo, Japan, 25 July 2015.

11 Lee, interview.

12 Lee, interview.

13 Lee, interview.

14 Lee, interview.

CHAPTER NINE

1 W. Somerset Maugham, *The Gentleman in the Parlour: A Record of a Journey from Rangoon to Haiphong* (1930; reprint, New York: Paragon House, 1989), 243-244.

2 "Singapore politics: Falling on their wallets," *The Economist*, January 7, 2012, 34.

3 Michael Malay, "Singapore needs to address its treatment of migrant workers," *The Guardian*, posted April 21, 2014. http://www.theguardian.com/global-development-professionals-network/2014/apr/21/singapore-address-treatment-migrant-workers.

4 John Gee, e-mail interview by author, June 20, 2010.

5 Elaine Huang, "Growing Number of Migrant Workers Stirs Debate in Singapore," *IPS Asia-Pacific*, posted March 18, 2013. http://aseannews.net/growing-number-of-migrant-workers-stirs-debate-in-singapore.

6 Kirsten Han, "Singapore's Exploited Immigrant Workers," *The Daily Beast*, posted November 8, 2013. http://www.thedailybeast.com/articles/2013/11/08/singapore-s-exploited-immigrant-workers.html.

7 "Singapore's Angry Migrant Workers," *New York Times*, December 27, 2013. http://www.nytimes.com/2013/12/28/opinion/singaore's-angry-migrant-workers.

8 Han, "Singapore's Exploited Immigrant Workers".

9 Sue-Ann Chia, "Civil servants to get bigger mid-year bonus," *The Straits Times*, Singapore, May 28, 2010, sec. A, p. 1.

10 Fiona Chan, "Factories crank up record growth," *The Straits Times*, Singapore, May 21, 2010, sec. A, p. 11.

11 Himiwari Minimart store owner, interview by author, Singapore, May 16, 2010.

12 Ang Peng Hwa, interview by author, Singapore, May 19, 2010.

13 Radha Basu, e-mail interview by author, June 16, 2010.

14 Radha Basu, "It's a raid—and men, rats, roaches scurry about," *The Straits Times*, Singapore, May 18, 2010, sec. A, p. 12.

15 Gee, e-mail interview by author, June 20, 2010.

16 Malay, "Singapore needs to address its treatment of migrant workers."

17 Abo Rhaman B Abo Samad, interview by author, Singapore, May 15, 2010.

18 "After the patriarch," *The Economist*, March 28, 2015, 44.

19 Huang, "Growing Number of Migrant Workers Stirs Debate in Singapore."

20 Joann Tan, e-mail interview by author, July 8, 2010.

21 Malay, "Singapore needs to address its treatment of migrant workers."

22 Huang, "Growing Number of Migrant Workers Stirs Debate in Singapore."

23 Gee, e-mail interview by author, June 20, 2010.

24 Basu, e-mail interview by author, June 16, 2010.

25 Brenda Yeoh and Weiqiang Lin, "Rapid Growth in Singapore's Immigrant Population Brings Policy Changes," *Migration Information Services*, Migration Policy Institute, April 3, 2012. http://www.migrationpolicy.org/article/rapid-growth-singapores.

26 Gee, e-mail interview by author, June 20, 2010.

INDEX

65167948R00076

Made in the USA
Charleston, SC
22 December 2016